The Invisible Hand
in Economics and Politics

*A Study in the Two Conflicting Explanations
of Society: End-States and Processes*

NORMAN P. BARRY

*Professor of Politics,
University of Buckingham*

Published by
THE INSTITUTE OF ECONOMIC AFFAIRS
1988

First published in August 1988

by

THE INSTITUTE OF ECONOMIC AFFAIRS
2 Lord North Street, Westminster,
London SW1P 3LB

© THE INSTITUTE OF ECONOMIC AFFAIRS 1988

Hobart Paper 111

ISSN 0073-2818
ISBN 0-255 36213-7

Printed in Great Britain by
GORON PRO-PRINT CO LTD
6 Marlborough Road, Churchill Industrial Estate, Lancing, W. Sussex
Text set in Berthold Baskerville

CONTENTS

		page
PREFACE	*Arthur Seldon*	7
THE AUTHOR		13
ACKNOWLEDGEMENTS		14
GLOSSARY		15
SYNOPSIS		19

I. TWO THEORIES OF SOCIETY: END-STATES
  AND PROCESSES   25
  End-state social theories   25
  Process and procedural theories   26
  Adam Smith's 'Invisible Hand' process theory   27
  The neglect of market processes   28

II. THREE END-STATE THEORIES   29
  A. The Notion of General Equilibrium   29
    Hahnian equilibrium   30
    Two kinds of equilibrium   31
    Dynamic equilibrium   32
    Limitations of equilibrium theory   33
    Implicit theory of normative economics   35
    Assumptions about human behaviour   36
  B. The Doctrine of Utilitarianism   37
    Bentham's 'felicific calculus'   38
    Keynesian macro-economic
      'act-utilitarianism'   39
    The inequality of utilitarianism   40
  C. The End-Goal of 'Social Justice'   41
    Efficiency or social justice?   42
    Summary   43

[3]

III. SELF-GENERATING AND SELF-CORRECTING
SOCIAL PROCESSES   44
  Unintended consequences—the
    evolutionary process   44
  Anti-rationalist generation of institutions   46
  Anti-rationalist, not irrationalist   47

IV. THE INVISIBLE HAND AS AN ECONOMIC PROCESS   49
  The failure of planning (UK) . . .   50
  . . . and the success of social market
    economy (W. Germany)   51
  'Human action, not human design'   51
  Common law v. statute law   53

V. THE SELF-CORRECTING PROCESS   54
  Time, the market and the Invisible Hand   55
  Pigou, Coase and social cost   56

VI. THE ERRORS OF MARKET SOCIALISM   58
  Entrepreneurial risk-taking = economic progress   59

VII. THE INVISIBLE HAND, JUSTICE AND WELFARE   60
  What is social justice?   60
  The 'catastrophic results' of unimpeded property
    rights (Sen)   61

VIII. PROPERTY AND JUSTICE   64
  Is there a 'just' distribution?   64

IX. SELF-INTEREST THE UNIVERSAL PRIME-MOVER   67
  Is the pursuit of self-interest counter-productive? 67
  Co-operative enterprise cannot be forced   69

X. POLITICAL v. ECONOMIC PROCESS   70
  The political process versus the market process   71
  A sovereign parliament leads to decline
    of liberalism   73

[4]

XI. THE IDEOLOGY OF THE POLITICAL PROCESS   75
       Group theories are anti-rationalist   75
       Pressure groups and free trade   77
       Constitutional reform *v.* 'elective dictatorship'   79
       No price mechanism in politics   80
       Discretionary political decisions harm efficiency
          and freedom   81

XII. CONCLUSION   83

TOPICS FOR GENERAL DISCUSSION AND
   QUESTIONS FOR STUDENTS   84

READINGS FOR FURTHER STUDY   86

SUMMARY   *Back cover*

[5]

PREFACE

The *Hobart Papers* were devised in 1960 to create a stream of authoritative, independent and lucid analyses of human action in industry and government. Since individual decisions of people for themselves as buyers and sellers in the market and their collective decisions for others they ostensibly 'represent' as politicians and bureaucrats in government are imperfect, the judgement between market and government, where they are alternatives for the production of goods and services, turns on the economic analysis of 'market failure' and 'government failure'.

Like Professor William Mitchell's Hobart Paper 109, *Government As It Is*, written by an American political scientist, Professor Norman Barry, a British political scientist, examines in Hobart Paper 111 the political process of collective decision-making and contrasts it with the results of individual decision-making in the market process. Both authors go to the roots of the fundamental principles, still misunderstood or ignored by most British (and American) economists and political scientists, that explain the differences between the formation and consequences of individual and collective decision-making.

The two *Hobart Papers* complement each other. Professor Mitchell argues that conventional political science as still studied and taught to students fails to explain the political process, and therefore why it would have to be refined by the *economic* analysis of politics—its costs and benefits to individual voter/taxpayers rather than the indeterminate and pretentious debates on the generalised collective and unpriced 'priorities' or 'needs' that form the staple of 'democratic' politics. Professor Barry now supplements this new kind of political science by contrasting the market as a continuing process with the conventional political study of society as an ideal goal or 'end-state'. His analysis of the distinction between the market process and the political process, his refutation of the argument for the 'end-state' theories of influential economists, and his conclusions for policy-making are summarised in the Synopsis (pp. 19-23).

Both *Hobart Papers* are thus two more studies of the basic

principles and structure of modern politico-economic society which have formed the bedrock of IEA analysis and prescription for reform in economic policy. In the years since 1957 some of the important 'practical' IEA *Papers* have examined the production of specific goods and services and pointed to market solutions. Resale price maintenance has passed into history. Advertising is no longer denigrated on principle (and indeed is used by former detractors). Hire purchase has become as respectable as home mortgages (and both are supplied by former critics in the clearing banks). The restrictive professions are judged no more politically untouchable than the trade unions. Proposals for introducing choice into state services are being closely examined. And charging for government services (thus revealing them as not 'public goods') is spreading. Yet the most essential IEA studies have been of the 'theoretical' basic principles and structures of individual and collective behaviour.

Among the most notable, and effective in their long-term effects on changing minds, have been those on the cult of 'growthmanship' at any price (Colin Clark), the false gods of 'national plans' (John Brunner) and 'incomes policies' (Samuel Brittan), the tiger of inflation (Frederick Hayek), the false god of government spending as the cure for unemployment (Alan Walters, Milton Friedman), the pitfalls of 'public choice' (J. M. Buchanan, Gordon Tullock), the delusions of 'social cost' (Stephen Cheung), the unique role and indispensability of the entrepreneur (Israel Kirzner), the political unreality of alternating budget deficits and surpluses (J. M. Buchanan, John Burton and Robert Wagner), the over-simplicities of the 'mixed economy' (S. C. Littlechild), and many more.

Together the 'theoretical' and 'practical' studies have over 30 years shown the long-neglected strengths of the market process and the long-ignored weaknesses of the political process. And the demonstration has re-inforced the inclination of recent government to implement policies hitherto misjudged as 'politically impossible'. The market is gradually being used (or not hindered) where it is superior to 'politics'. Desocialisation, renamed privatisation, has become commonplace in Britain, gradually accepted in all political parties, and has spread overseas. The market, formerly anathematised, is advocated without the risk of instant political suicide and instead embraced with prospect of electoral reward, not least from the newly-emancipated 'working-classes', despite uninformed priestly displeasure.

The relationship between the 'theoretical' and 'practical' *Papers* has formed the kernel of IEA intellectual strategy. In the two-century battle of ideas between the four decisive schools of economic thought personified by Adam Smith, Karl Marx, J. M. Keynes and Frederick Hayek, the fallacies have had to be demolished before better thinking was accepted. It was the intellectual 'artillery' bombardment of 'theory' that destroyed opposing fallacies before the 'infantry' of proposals for practical reform could take demoralised opposing positions. The strategy of the military commander and the cricket captain inspired the parallels for the economic contest in the arguments for the state and the market.

This is the fundamental background to Professor Barry's *Paper*. He examines and contests the continuing critique of the market from the academic world that lags long behind both popular preference for the market-based 'capitalist' system and its belated acceptance and advocacy by politicians in all parties since 1979. He deals mainly with the writings of Professors F. H. Hahn of Cambridge. A. K. Sen of Harvard, Gerard Debreu of California (Berkeley), and K. J. Arrow of Stanford. But there are still many other critics, and they will continue to influence a generation of students who will reflect fallacious teaching in their working lives into the 21st century. The latest example is the recent Marxist-overweighted successor to the celebrated 1890s *Palgrave Dictionary of Political Economy*, edited by economists at Cambridge, Harvard and Johns Hopkins Universities (J. Eatwell, M. Milgate, P. Newman, published by Macmillan, 1987). And the nostalgia for the teachings of Keynes is still echoed by older economists, like Professor James Tobin of Yale, in the remarkably balanced hour-long video written and presented by Professor Mark Blaug, *J. M. Keynes: Life, Ideas, Legacy* (IEA, 1988).

Professor Barry's *Hobart Paper* thus continues the intellectual debate between the state and the market since Adam Smith. There can by now be little doubt that, except among older economists won to Keynesian thinking in their youth, or younger economists who derive their distaste for liberal 'capitalism' by contrasting it with an unrealisable vision of benevolent collectivism, the market has largely vanquished the state in argument and evidence. But the tasks of replacing the state and its supporting intellectual and vested interests will remain stubborn. Not the least task will be to break out of the vicious

[9]

circle in which the political process progressively extends its writ. Politicians and bureaucrats have a natural professional interest in preserving their political province. 'The invisible hand' that leads individuals in the market unintentionally to serve the public interest seems in politics to thwart the public interest. And even where politicians are influenced by new thinking, recent history since 1979 shows the power of vested interests, at least in the short run, to resist their new-found inclinations. Contemporary history reveals the stubborn paradox that politicians who wish to liberate the individual from the dominion of politics by enlarging choice in the market end after nine years by taking even more of individual income and subjecting it to the precarious collective decision-making of politics. The conundrum remains to be solved by the study of the economics of 'public choice'.

Yet an encouraging exemplar is to be found not too far away in Europe. Once it was the social market economy of West Germany. Sweden maintains economic markets and political liberty but at the high price of individual enervation in a pervasive welfare state. The best lessons lie in Switzerland, which properly reduces its politicians to almost anonymous administrators of the essentials of government. There is a long way to go.

These fundamental issues in the nature of politico-economic systems require to be analysed in largely abstract terms that are more easily absorbed by economists than by beginners in the subject or by non-economists accustomed to think in more concrete terms. Several such IEA *Papers* over the years have discussed the implications of macro-economic thinking for policy in the market economy (Professor L. M. Lachmann), the fallacies in the so-called Cambridge Revolution in economic thought (Professor Mark Blaug), and the replacement of state monopoly by private competition in the supply of money (Professor F. A. Hayek). There, and in other *Papers*, newcomers to economics were advised to read the text more than once to see the importance of the argument. Professor Barry's discussion is necessarily abstract and requires close reading, especially to follow the refinements in the reasoning, on which professional economists and political scientists may differ even where they broadly concur in the eventual implications for the choice between the state and the market. The Synopsis (pp. 19-23) and the Glossary (pp. 15-18) will help such readers.

[10]

The Institute has to thank Professors S. C. Littlechild and Albert Weale and Dr Cento Veljanovski for reactions to an early draft that the author has borne in mind in his final revisions. Its constitution requires it to dissociate its Trustees, Advisers and Directors from the analyses of the authors, but it presents Professor Barry's *Hobart Paper* as a timely contribution to the unabated intellectual battle on the roles of the state and the market that underlies the national and international controversies and events of our day.

*   *   *

This Preface is the last of my 250 written to put into context the work of some 300 IEA authors. I am especially glad to end with the *Hobart Papers* by Professors Mitchell and Barry because the outcome of the contest of the state and the market will turn on the degree to which the polity can be subjected to the economy. And both authors are political scientists whose analyses go to the roots of the economic debate.

In choosing authors for IEA Papers over 30 years, often with the assistance of the academic advisers, I sometimes felt like the manager of a cricket team putting the best players in to 'bat' against the opposing sides. Historians will judge the effects of the long academic debate on public and political opinion, as seen in the intellectual and cultural revolution between the 1950s, when the market was anathema, and the 1980s, when it is being offered by every political party, old and new, and in the resurgence of Britain and the West against the decaying cult of the state in the East and the Third World.

April/May 1988   ARTHUR SELDON

THE AUTHOR

NORMAN BARRY is Professor of Politics at the University of Buckingham. He was previously Senior Lecturer in Government at the City of Birmingham Polytechnic, and he has taught at the University of Exeter and the Queen's University of Belfast.

His research interests are in political philosophy, political economy, the foundations of classical liberalism, and public policy.

His books include *Hayek's Social and Economic Philosophy* (1979), *An Introduction to Modern Political Theory* (1981), and *The New Right* (1987), and he has written extensively in academic journals. He is a regular contributor to the IEA journal, *Economic Affairs*.

He is a Trustee of the David Hume Institute, Edinburgh.

Some of the material in the following paper is a development of his articles, 'In Defence of the Invisible Hand', *Cato Journal*, 5 (1985) and 'A Defence of Liberalism against Politics', *Indian Journal of Political Science*, Vol. 41 (1980), and of his Inaugural Lecture, 'End-States, Processes and Politics', delivered at the University of Buckingham in December 1985.

ACKNOWLEDGEMENTS

I should like to thank Dr John Gray, Jesus College, Oxford, and Professor Martin Ricketts, University of Buckingham, for their helpful advice and comments on an earlier version of this *Paper*. Also, I am grateful to Professor Mark Blaug, Universities of Buckingham and London, for his valuable comments on the economic aspects of the work. Much as I would like to implicate these eminent scholars in the final version, I fear I cannot. Also, I am indebted to Arthur Seldon for steering the *Paper* through its various stages with his customary rigour.

When I discovered that this was the last *Hobart Paper* to be edited by Arthur, I felt deeply honoured and not a little saddened. Less than expert exponents of the free market and users of the English language may have occasionally experienced just a little frustration at his pertinacity, but even the most accomplished would not deny that their understanding of these two beautiful and spontaneously evolving phenomena has been improved immeasurably by his meticulous attention to the nuances and intricacies of both. We shall remember him with the deepest affection.

June 1988   N.P.B.

GLOSSARY

COMPARATIVE STATICS—A technique of analysis which attempts to show the effect of a change on an economy by comparing two states of rest (or equilibria): one before the change, one after.

DEDUCTION—A deductive argument uses the form of reasoning in which the conclusion *necessarily* follows from the premises. The validity of a deductive argument is established if it is impossible to assert the premises and deny the conclusion without self-contradiction. In the social sciences only economic theory makes extensive use of the deductive method.

EPISTEMOLOGY—The theory of knowledge. The main questions of epistemology concern the nature of our knowledge of the external world, the source of knowledge and the roles of reason and experience in substantiating claims to knowledge. Economists are interested in the type of knowledge contained in a market system and how it can be explained.

EVENLY ROTATING ECONOMY—The expression used by Ludwig von Mises to describe a market in a state of rest with no incentive to change—'equilibrium'. In an evenly rotating economy output is reproduced continually in an identical form. For Mises it was not meant to describe existing economies, which are always characterised by change and uncertainty, but how they functioned as a theoretical entity. It was useful to the extent that human action shows a tendency to equilibrium.

EXHAUSTIBLE RESOURCES—Resources such as oil and minerals which are in finite supply. They may be contrasted with resources which are not depleted by constant use, e.g. solar power or wind power. Some economists believe that, at current consumption rates, exhaustible resources can be predicted to run out at a definite point in the future, and therefore their use must be 'rationed'. Market economists argue that this is not a problem because the price mechanism automatically regulates their use; as they are depleted their prices simply rise.

EXTERNALITIES—The unintended effects on third parties, or the community at large, of the actions of market traders. Externalities may be harmful or beneficial. The most frequently cited example of a harmful externality is pollution of the natural environment caused by producers using the least-cost methods of production. Since such externalities cannot be priced by the normal market mechanism, the market is said to 'fail'. Contemporary market theorists maintain that externalities could be 'internalised' if property rights were more adequately defined, so that those harmed could sue for damages.

FELICIFIC CALCULUS—The quasi-technical term invented by Jeremy Bentham to describe how pleasures are to be measured and compared so that particular policies can be evaluated and the policy that maximises the greatest amount of (objective) pleasure should be implemented by a legislator. Pleasure was thought to be measured along seven dimensions. Since it is a subjective phenomenon and incapable of measurement, and policies therefore cannot be compared and evaluated objectively, such a calculus was never taken seriously.

NORMATIVE—The word used for propositions that contain 'value-judgements': statements about the (ethical) desirability of certain states of affairs. Normative economic arguments are to be contrasted with *positive* economics, which describes economic phenomena and searches for causal laws that explain the connection between one event and another. Normative propositions declare what 'should' be, positive propositions what 'is'.

PARETO-OPTIMUM—This exists when the allocation of resources in an economy is such that there can be no re-allocation which does not make (at least) one person worse off. It is used as a criterion of social welfare. It is a relatively weak criterion since in an existing economy a Pareto-improvement is possible only where a change benefits (at least) one person and leaves everybody else as they were before. Since the Pareto principle prohibits inter-personal comparison of utilities, any change which benefited some substantially and harmed one person only minutely would not qualify as an increase in social welfare. Furthermore, the Pareto criterion is silent on the distribution of property rights from which Pareto-improvements can be made.

POSITIONAL GOODS—They are goods, the supply of which does not expand as demand rises. This limitation need not be merely physical or a function of pure scarcity, as in a beautiful landscape or rare works of art. It could also be social, for example, when a person derives satisfaction from being the sole owner of a good or the occupant of some status position.

POSITIVISM—The doctrine that upholds a rigid distinction between values and facts. Positivist economists want to eliminate all value statements from economic theory. Some extreme positivists believe that *all* theoretical statements which cannot be empirically tested should be eliminated from economics. However, some economists, especially 'Austrians', accept the fact/value distinction but deny that the only scientific theories in economics are those that can be tested.

PUBLIC GOODS—Goods and services which cannot be supplied by the normal market mechanisms. This is because they display the features of 'non-rivalness' (the consumption of the good by one person does not reduce the supply for others, as with information transmitted by a lighthouse), and 'non-excludability' (once the good is supplied it can be consumed by everybody at zero cost so that there is the 'free-rider' problem). Classic examples of public goods like defence provide the economist with a rationale for state intervention. The theory of public goods has the same logic as the theory of externalities.

PRISONER'S DILEMMA—A situation in which, although rational self-interested action by individuals produces social outcomes not desired by them, there are no incentives for them to behave in any other way. For example, if land is held in common with each individual having an unrestricted right to use it, its fertility will quickly be exhausted. The phenomenon occurs in market systems in the supply of public goods but is just as likely to occur in mixed economies where individual self-interested support for state intervention is, ultimately, socially destructive.

SOCIAL DARWINISM—The 19th-century sociological and political doctrine that applied Darwin's biological theory, that evol-

[17]

ution proceeds by natural selection, directly to society. Social institutions are explained in terms of a 'survival of the fittest' process: those that decay do so because they fail to adapt to circumstances. In Britain and the USA it was often used by extreme *laissez-faire* theorists to oppose state intervention on the ground that it hindered the processes of natural selection.

SOCIAL WELFARE FUNCTION—This is normally interpreted as a rule for ranking alternative social states. In an ethical rather than a formal mathematical sense, it states the objectives, such as utility or social justice, which public policy should aim at promoting. Many market economists believe that, since all choice is subjective, any social welfare function is no more than the imposition of one person's (or group's) values on the community as a whole.

SYNOPTIC DELUSION—The belief that the human mind is capable of knowing all the facts relevant to the understanding of any situation. In social affairs it is exemplified by the aim of comprehensive rational economic planning. In contrast, liberal economics emphasises the de-centralised nature of knowledge.

TORT—A civil wrong, such as negligence, that does not arise out of contract, for which the remedy is damages.

UTILITY—The concept was originally (from Jeremy Bentham) identified with measurable pleasure and social and economic policies were desirable to the extent that they maximised a sum of pleasures. This approach was thought by some utilitarians to be a 'science' of public policy. Market economists claim that pleasure is not cardinally measurable (as if it were temperature on a thermometer) and that inter-personal comparisons are unscientific. Utility is a subjective phenomenon and the word is used as a label to describe individual well-being, with no social implications. However, social theorists use the concept in a looser ethical sense to describe the beneficial *consequences* that emerge from certain policies but do not claim that it has any objective status.

N.P.B.

SYNOPSIS

Two schools of politico-economic thought have produced conflicting theories (explanations) of how society works. They have fundamental and far-reaching consequences for practical policy in everyday life. This *Hobart Paper* examines the two very different ways in which economists and political philosophers understand society and the associated systems of values.

The long-established way of understanding society is by envisaging the final goal of policy and analysing the resulting 'end-state' of public activity and politics. This approach constructs an 'ideal' economic (and sometimes ethical) system and proceeds to evaluate or judge existing societies according to how far they conform to, or fall short of, the ideal. It envisages society as the creation of a more or less centralised authority.

The newer, alternative, economic approach is to see society as a continuing 'process' of interaction and exchange between individuals that does not lead to a predictable final goal or 'end-state'. This decentralised activity, it is claimed, is likely to produce a smoother (although not necessarily more 'efficient') interaction and co-ordination of human activity than government direction or planning designed to produce a pre-determined state.

The ability of the two contrasting economic theories to interpret the idea of an exchange society is of special importance because the various attempts of economists and political scientists to unravel the mysteries of the market have fundamental implications for public policy and therefore for the well-being of the people.

The 'end-state' approach of the social world has both economic and political (or political/ethical) aspects. In political economy the emphasis has been on a state of equilibrium—in which the activities of buyers and sellers are co-ordinated to the point where all intentions or decisions are satisfied and there are no wasteful elements such as monopoly. In liberal political economy since Adam Smith the equilibrium state has been said to be created by a metaphorical 'invisible hand' which guides individuals to serve others *unintentionally* by serving themselves.

In modern economics there has been a relatively new emphasis on the mathematical proof of the existence of such an equilibrium rather than on the market process that produces the tendency to approach it. From Leon Walras, the French economist (1834-1910) who founded the theory of equilibrium, to present-day economists Debreu, Arrow and Hahn, the mathematical inquiry into the properties of an equilibrium has been wholly abstract, with no necessary practical implications for real-world public policy. Debreu has recently warned[1] economists and the outside world that the mathematical approach 'may be tempted to forget economic content and to shun economic problems that are not readily amenable to mathematization'. Some economists, especially the so-called market socialists who believe, contrary to economic analysis and without evidence of practical example, that centralised socialism can be reconciled with decentralised markets, have nevertheless used the notion of equilibrium as a desirable state of affairs against which existing capitalist (though, oddly, not existing socialist) economies may or should be judged.

The notion of equilibrium is an implicitly 'end-state' theory of the structure of society. The more explicitly political/ethical 'end-state' doctrines are those of 'utilitarianism' and the theory of 'social justice'.

The utilitarian approach judges a society as good to the extent that it maximises a 'sum' of pleasures. The social justice approach concludes with an ideal distribution of income different from that which emerges from the market. The argument here is that both theories are logically flawed and that the attempt to impose utilitarian or social justice end-states threatens to destroy not only the economic benefits of the co-ordinating processes of market exchange but also the moral values of individual liberty. Behind these superficially benign end-state doctrines lies the threat of dictatorship, benevolent or authoritarian.

In contrast, market processes are much more consonant with Adam Smith's original Invisible Hand explanation of free society. The *Paper* argues that the market is never in a state of equilibrium but always in an unending process of change as individual buyers and sellers adjust their decisions to the fluctuating data of the prices of goods, services, labour, capital,

[1] In the 1987 successor to the original 1890s Palgrave *Dictionary of Economics*, edited by Eatwell, Milgate and Newman, and published by Macmillan.

land and everything else. The price system thus does not, as its critics assert, represent at any point in time a state of perfect co-ordination but a continuing signalling mechanism which makes for co-ordination by transmitting price information that is necessarily dispersed and decentralised in modern Western civilised society. And, as the sad experience of socialist/communist systems that have attempted to dispense with pricing has eloquently demonstrated, the end-result is both privation and coercion.

In this market process the crucial role in creating co-ordination is played by the entrepreneur—the innovator, initiator, industrialist, businessman, large or small; their search for reward ('profit') by identifying and 'exploiting' differences in prices leads them (unintentionally, as Adam Smith emphasised) to reconcile and co-ordinate what would otherwise be (and in market-less societies generally is) unco-ordinated behaviour. Process theories thus centre on the motivations of individuals and the structures of institutions that together make for the *tendency* to equilibrium. This formulation of the Invisible Hand explanation of modern complex society does not represent an abstract ideal of efficiency but a co-ordination of human action which, although indirectly, is superior to its alternatives—the various forms of 'planned', centralised, *dirigiste* systems.

The contemporary move towards free markets in many Western countries, especially in the successful experience of the West German 'social market' economy, the remarkable results in the Far East, and the still more recent return to forms of markets in the communist world, have persuaded former critics of the Invisible Hand that it has unique wealth-creating properties. But they now say that these allocative advantages of efficiency in the market are bought at the high cost of unacceptable inequality and failure to produce acceptable standards of welfare.

It is true that, since the quantitative or qualitative outcomes of the market process cannot be known in advance, these deficiencies cannot be excluded in principle. But the criticism overlooks the very effect of the market, if left open for free movement between occupations, industries and regions, in tending towards equalisation of incomes and rewards. It also ignores the characteristic of the market that differences in profits, wages, salaries, are a necessary part of the system in signalling shortages and superfluities of abilities and skills.

[21]

Some critics, such as Professor A. K. Sen of Harvard, say that the untrammelled operation of free exchange may produce 'catastrophes': famines, for example, occur despite adequate food supplies, when the inviolability of property rights prevents a redistribution by the state. But this is not a criticism of the market in principle; such 'catastrophes' may be true only in extreme and exceptional cases of the Invisible Hand. In principle the market system requires private property rights, but private property can be given away in crises such as famine, flood or other natural calamity; and in the real world they usually are: it is the market economies that come to the rescue of the non-market economies. And the evidence of recent years is that catastrophes occur more frequently in the *dirigiste* economies.

Market economies require a framework of laws and politics to operate efficiently. The Invisible Hand process operates in the legal system as well as in economic relationships, especially in the spontaneous development of the Common Law as new cases reveal new circumstances that require new law. But some form of 'public' or political regulation of economic life through government is also required for the so-called 'public goods', such as defence, that cannot be produced in the market. The processes of politics in democratic societies based on the election of 'representatives' bear a resemblance to the processes of the market (although political motivations produce different results from economic motivations in the market). The political competition for votes and the bargaining between groups are, in a technical sense, processes that are the reverse of the imposition of 'rational plans' or end-states.

The important difference between the market process and the political process is that the Invisible Hand produces less benign consequences in the political process. The important reason for the difference is that there is no *immediate* budget constraint in politics, so that political action through representative institutions such as British Parliaments can impose burdens on the citizen that no individual who stands to lose has a strong enough motive to oppose and prevent. The unwelcome result is that the strong influence of group interests on politics in British and other Western societies has almost made them exempt from the rule of law and created departures from economic rationality that have undermined the public interest. The lax constitutional control of temporary legislatures in most Western democracies has permitted if not incited an enervating 'politicisation' of economic life.

The conclusion is that the form of politics most consonant with the preservation of a free society is that produced by 'constitutional politics'. The actions of government must be limited by much stricter rules than are applied now, so that government requires wider popular consent for the application of its powers.

N.P.B.

I. TWO THEORIES OF SOCIETY:
END-STATES AND PROCESSES

In the last twenty years social, economic and political theorists have analysed society by analogy either with an 'end-state' (or final outcome) or a 'process' (a chain of causes and consequences). Although these approaches are primarily methodological they have lessons for practical economic and public policy, outlined and illustrated in the course of this *Hobart Paper*. An understanding of freedom, equity and other social values depends very much on how we explain the mechanics of social order. And the role that politics plays in social life can be illuminated by the concepts of 'end-state' and 'process'.

End-state social theories

First, an end-state social theory attempts an understanding of social phenomena through a description of the features of a society at a specified point in time.[1] It is a kind of photograph which reveals such elements as a society's distribution of income, wealth, power, prestige, status, the structures of the economic and political systems, and so forth. It is as if a society were like a video film which we 'freeze frame' at certain points to discover its structural features. Both analogies illustrate the *static* character of end-state analyses. They do not show how a particular end-state or 'outcome' (I use the two terms interchangeably) comes about; nor do they describe the mechanisms that are to determine future changes. Nevertheless, in economic theory at least there is an attempt to show how the actions of decentralised agents, buyers and sellers or savers and investors, motivated by self-interest, are co-ordinated. An economic end-state does have an explanation or rationale.

Nevertheless, this limitation by no means precludes the end-state theorist from evaluating theory and policy. The economist or political philosopher is quite likely to have a picture of a more desirable end-state than the existing set of social and economic

[1] Robert Sugden, *The Political Economy of Public Choice*, Martin Robertson, Oxford, 1981, pp. 11-17, presents a similar and more detailed analysis.

arrangements; perhaps one that is more efficient or socially just. In theory, a free competitive market is said to generate an efficient end-state but in practice there may be (alterable) impediments to the achievement of this outcome. However, in the absence of an account of the processes and procedures by which this more desirable outcome can be reached, the implication of end-state theory is that attractive 'outcomes' may be better achieved by political methods. The political methods, in principle, are used to create an end-state which is in the general interests of society rather than of politicians. The ideals of 'managed capitalism'—social justice, and a 'welfare state'—are examples of end-states which are thought by economists or political philosophers to be intrinsically right. Liberalism, the economic and social system which makes individual choice decisive in the production of goods and services and private property the prevailing form of ownership, may also paradoxically be seen as an end-state if it is imposed on a community.

Process and procedural theories

In contrast, 'process' theories are much more concerned with how end-states or outcomes emerge spontaneously without collective action and human 'planning'. They may also be called procedural theories, since they are pre-eminently concerned with the nature of the rules in an orderly, regularised society; acting and choosing individuals who follow them can be said to generate certain end-states. The question asked is not 'What are the features of a particular outcome?' but rather 'How did it come about?' We may indeed 'freeze frame' at some points but we will wind the film back to see how the particular outcome emerged. Market mechanisms, legal systems and democratic and other political orders are examples of such processes. Social scientists who analyse processes that produce end-states are especially interested in *constitutions*. Their evaluation will thus not be confined to the end-state itself but will focus essentially on the procedural rules and human actions that generated it. Is a market exchange process efficient? Are the procedural rules that govern it acceptable? Are human rights violated in the operation of the process? Thus economists and political philosophers ask questions about justice as well as questions about efficiency.

Theories that explain process and procedural rules are rather more elusive than end-state theories. There are two subtly different types of procedural theories. One is *entirely* 'neutral'

[26]

about the character of end-states that may emerge from a process, the other less so.

This distinction is of some considerable theoretical interest. Those theories that are entirely neutral about the outcomes of a process or a procedure, whether it be a market system or a general social and legal system, are in effect saying that the human mind is incapable of making judgements about, say, 'efficiency' or the correct distribution of income. Some market economists, for example the public-choice theorist James Buchanan (winner of the Nobel Prize for Economic Science, 1986), would argue that it is impossible to compare various 'states of affairs'; instead the social scientist should concentrate exclusively on those rules and procedures under which individual economic agents interact (or exchange) with one another.[1] The value of an economic system varies with the extent to which it maximises individual choice and not its consistency or otherwise with some 'imaginary' efficient state of affairs. If there is to be state intervention it must be decreed by a constitutional procedure (but normally a much more rigorous one than simple majority-rule democracy) which reflects individual choice rather than imposed by a benevolent economic 'dictator' informed by a rational plan of economic efficiency. A political or economic reform should therefore be directed towards the improvement of constitutional procedures.

Adam Smith's 'Invisible Hand' process theory

Most theorists, however, favour particular processes and procedures which they think are most likely to produce generally acceptable outcomes—in comparison at least to the actions of benevolent dictators. The most famous process theory in the history of thought—Adam Smith's 'Invisible Hand' hypothesis—is certainly of this type. Adam Smith wrote (in 1776) of a metaphorical 'Invisible Hand' that guides people to an *end* which is no part of their intention. He meant that an impersonal market, operating through price signals, will allocate resources more efficiently and thence ensure general prosperity better than the deliberate intentions even of benevolent dictators. He was, however, like most other social process theorists, prepared to concede that the Invisible Hand did not always operate so

[1] J. M. Buchanan, *The Limits of Liberty*, University of Chicago Press, Chicago, 1975.

felicitously and that some intervention was required to supplement pure spontaneity.[1]

The main thrust of the theory is thus that market processes, in the form of voluntary exchange between decentralised buyers and sellers, are more likely to produce an efficient outcome than the designs of rational planners.

The neglect of market processes

The argument of this *Hobart Paper* is that economists have neglected the self-correcting processes of the market because of their over-emphasis on the description of a perfectly co-ordinating end-state. And it has led them to the view that desirable end-states can be created more effectively by political action by government.

Three examples of end-state theories are familiar to economists and social philosophers but not to other specialists in the social sciences or to laymen. They are:

(i) the notion of general equilibrium;

(ii) the doctrine of utilitarianism; and

(iii) the contemporary goal of 'social' justice.

An analysis of these three end-state theories reveals two inter-connected properties. First, they are 'rationalistic', in the sense that the human mind is deemed to be superior to natural social processes so that 'reason' can prescribe institutional forms irrespective of the lessons of experience. Secondly, they trade heavily on a peculiar view of 'knowledge': that it can be centralised and stated entirely in the form of propositions for practical action by government. Both are fallacious. Much of post-war social and economic policy in Western democracies proceeds from these two fallacies.

[1] Book V of *The Wealth of Nations*, ed. by R. H. Campbell and A. S. Skinner, Clarendon Press, Oxford, 1976. Adam Smith did not speculate on the forms or procedures which should govern state intervention.

[28]

II. THREE END-STATE THEORIES

A. THE NOTION OF GENERAL EQUILIBRIUM

The idea that the existence of multi-market equilibrium is *the* economic problem derives from the work of the French economist Leon Walras in the 1870s. It has been perfected in modern times by the American economist Kenneth Arrow, the French-American economist Gerard Debreu and the Cambridge economist Frank Hahn. In modern economic analysis general equilibrium theorists have been concerned to prove that the working of Adam Smith's imaginary Invisible Hand does generate a social and economic optimum—a state of perfect co-ordination of economic activity. But modern equilibrium theory tries to show that, although it is possible to demonstrate mathematically that an equilibrium (a state of affairs in which no individual has an incentive to change) can exist, it may not necessarily be an efficient one because of the presence of 'market failure'. An efficient equilibrium, it is argued, is a desirable end-state but an unaided market process, at least that described by Adam Smith and his successors, may require considerable state intervention if it is to be achieved. It is said that the economic potential of a community cannot be exploited by the market process alone.

Such critics of the Invisible Hand do not generally want to amputate the limb and replace it with a superior steering device but to expose the infirmities in its joints and muscles and indicate some unsureness of its grasp. The existence of monopolies in imperfectly competitive markets is often cited as an example of the failure of the Invisible Hand. Another is the familiar instance of 'externalities' in the form of pollution of the environment. There is also the logically similar problem of the market's inability to supply 'public goods', for example, defence, law and order. What differentiates this approach from Adam Smith's and his successors' method is not the problem of market failure, a phenomenon of which he was well aware, but his emphasis on the *processes* by which an hypothetical equilibrium is approached contrasted with the critics' description of the end-state itself.

Some economists' criticism of existing markets extends

[29]

beyond the question of efficiency. They argue that the market mechanism, with its associated properties of individual self-interest and apparently arbitrary distribution of property rights, produces a morally unacceptable distribution of wealth-riches for the few while many are in poverty. Furthermore, the notion of self-interest itself has been criticised as inadequate to explain the success of some nominally capitalist economies, such as Japan. In these subjects the voice of Amartya Sen, the Harvard University economist, has been the most eloquent (below, pp. 60-66).

The proponents of the market do not reject the equilibrium concept entirely. Indeed, the very discovery that there are tendencies towards equilibrium in economic society made possible an economic science of human behaviour. Furthermore, market economists have produced good reasons to show that, when left to themselves, and under specified conditions such as the impartial application of rules of just conduct (property, crime, contract and tort), individuals will co-ordinate their actions. But the discovery that under some circumstances a free market may not work so felicitously and that corrective action by political methods is required, has had the (unintended?) consequence of licensing all sorts of political action in human activities where it is far from appropriate (below, pp. 70-80). The problem has been compounded by the concern of many professional economists to describe theoretically the technical properties of an end-state equilibrium rather than to elucidate the causal processes that produce it.

Hahnian Equilibrium

Although Professor Hahn's most distinguished work in equilibrium theory is in mathematical form (indeed, the representation of equilibrium in mathematics is one of the finest technical achievements of the human mind), he has presented logically similar conclusions in some literary essays easily accessible to the non-mathematical mind. I shall draw mainly on his 1982 Fred Hirsch Memorial Lecture and two other essays.[1] He is not always clear what he means by 'equilibrium'; he uses the concept in slightly different senses, and it is not obvious what policy implications he draws from them.

[1] F. Hahn, 'Reflections on the Invisible Hand', *Lloyds Bank Review*, April 1982; 'The Winter Of Our Discontent', *Economica*, 40 (1973); *On the Notion of Equilibrium in Economics*, Cambridge University Press, Cambridge, 1973. Also his *Equilibrium and Macroeconomics*, Blackwell, Oxford, 1984.

In his Fred Hirsch Lecture, Hahn appears to be describing the 'pure theory' of the Invisible Hand as an equilibrium theory. An economic system is presented as a perfect co-ordination of economic actions in which the price structure allows no possibility of further profitable advantages. According to Hahn:

> 'The economic environment of any one person is fully specified once the prices of all tradeable objects are given. These prices are the terms at which one good can be exchanged for another and it is a basic assumption that all individuals can trade to any extent they wish at these prices. One notices that the economic information is conveyed very economically—the individual knows everything that he needs to know once he knows prices.'[1]

Hahn assumes that all individuals are price-takers (no one person can influence price), they are endowed with perfect knowledge of all supplies and prices, and markets are 'complete', that is, all goods and services are tradeable at known prices in all periods of time, present and future (there are futures markets in all goods and services). They then react in the manner of automatons to their environment, and their actions can be predicted by an external observer. These acts are, in Hahn's words, 'machine-like responses of agents to prices'.[2] The theoretical argument, therefore, for the operation of the Invisible Hand is reduced to the abstract *mathematical* proof of the proposition that in a world of decentralised trading there exists a set of equilibrium prices at which the actions of buyers and sellers will 'mesh'; there will be no dis-co-ordination to be corrected by further trading. It is also crucial to Hahn's conception that in this abstract model of a market individuals do not make *mistakes*. It might be thought that this notion is 'unrealistic', but the objection would be irrelevant because the aim is to provide a mathematical proof of the possible existence of an equilibrium rather than an assertion that it must exist. Whether this technical exercise has any practical utility I consider below (pp. 49-53).

Two kinds of equilibrium

A slightly different statement of Hahn's position on equilibrium can be found in his earlier essays,[3] where two sorts of

---

[1] F. Hahn, 'Reflections on the Invisible Hand', *op. cit.*, p. 2.

[2] *Ibid.*, p. 6.

[3] Especially *On the Notion of Equilibrium in Economics*, *op. cit.*

equilibrium are differentiated: the timeless static world described in the above model and a more dynamic version in which the sequential movement of an economy is explored. Perhaps no *direct* policy conclusions follow from the two representations, but an accurate treatment of Hahn's views requires that they be examined.

The more dynamic version is more interesting. Professor S. C. Littlechild has pointed out that it has much in common with the Hayekian version of equilibrium.[1] It represents a significant departure from the conventional model for, instead of using equilibrium theory to represent or 'objectify' a static and unchanging picture of perfect co-ordination, it addresses the question of how individuals, through a *learning* process, adjust their plans through time so as to reach the equilibrium state. This 'subjectivist' view of economics sees the task of equilibrium theory as one of incorporating an explanation of individual action in a less rarefied world than that of comparative statics. Hahn puts the matter accurately when he says that this theory

'requires that information processes and costs, and also expectations and uncertainty, be essentially included in the equilibrium notion. This is what the Arrow-Debreu construction does *not* do'.[2]

Dynamic equilibrium

In Hahn's model, economic action is seen as sequential action; each individual has a notion of how the economy will develop over time, and his theory will be altered (through the learning process) in accordance with his perception of changes in the data that confront him. If every change is correctly foreseen, each individual is in equilibrium: and an economy is in equilibrium when all the individual theories or plans are mutually compatible. Hayek had used a similar dynamic notion of equilibrium in his *The Pure Theory of Capital*.[3] Hahn's dynamic equilibrium is a modification or re-statement of the static model, which, since it envisages a once-and-for-all state of affairs, does not attempt to accommodate change.

An example may be helpful in illustrating the differences between the two concepts of equilibrium used by Hahn. Imagine

[1] S. C. Littlechild, 'Equilibrium and Market Process', in Israel Kirzner (ed.), *Method, Process and Austrian Economics*, D. C. Heath, Lexington, Mass., 1982.

[2] *On the Notion of Equilibrium in Economics, op. cit.*, p. 16.

[3] Routledge & Kegan Paul, London, 1941, Ch.II.

a producer with special knowledge of future weather conditions. He knows that it will be *unusually* hot at a certain time of the year; so he buys up quantities of cheap materials to manufacture summer clothes. Since he is the first into the market, he will secure a 'profit'—a surplus over and above the income required to keep his labour efficiently employed. In the static equilibrium model, however, *other* transactors will have this knowledge and correctly forecast the future prices of lightweight clothes; the prices of the raw materials will therefore be (instantaneously) bid up to equilibrium level, so eliminating profit.

In the modified version of equilibrium, the claim is that we cannot know the future with the degree of certainty that instantaneous adjustment would require, and therefore, presumably, mistakes will be made. The buyers and sellers will, however, be influenced by the idea that there is an equilibrium solution to a co-ordination problem. There is an end-state of perfect co-ordination in the market *which the economist can identify*. But it is not at all clear that Hahn's modified version improves our understanding of how real markets work, that it contributes to an explanation of the Invisible Hand theory. It still does not include a discussion of the mechanisms, such as 'profit', emphasised by the market process theorists, which drive the system. Indeed, there is little or no analysis of the institutional framework within which economic action takes place. Hahn himself admits that his kind of equilibrium economists do not have a theory of the learning process at all.

Limitations of equilibrium theory

The crucial point is that Hayek sees more clearly the *limitations* of equilibrium theory, as Mises did before him in his *Nationalökonomie: Theorie des Handelns und Wirtschaftens* (1940)[1] (though the Misesian construction of an 'evenly rotating economy' does not accommodate change, it can be used as a bench-mark against which we can understand change). A theory of equilibrium is a deliberate abstraction from reality, a limiting case, which enables us to understand how and in what ways the behaviour of real economies departs from the theoretical model. Thus, far from extending and refining the basic postulates of equilibrium theory so that they provide a truer picture of reality, Hayek, in a series of important essays written in the early post-

[1] This important work was expanded and translated into English as *Human Action*, University of Chicago Press, Chicago, 1949.

war years,[1] goes on to take account of other economic mechanisms which are ignored in contemporary micro-economic thought. Notable here, of course, is entrepreneurship (completely absent from any equilibrium model), which explains how an economy tends to move toward the state of perfect co-ordination described by abstract theory.

Hahn has often said that further progress in economic science can come only from the continual refinement of the general equilibrium model (though he does not believe that economics is exhausted by it). While accepting that it does not reflect reality, he claims that: 'The student of general equilibrium believes that he has a starting point from which it is possible to advance towards a *descriptive* theory'.[2] Thus he is less interested in economic processes, genuine competition, entrepreneurship, or innovation, all of which characterise real economies, than in routine, regularised, and repetitive behaviour that can be encapsulated in equations that have no bearing on the real world at all. Yet the most casual observation of economic develop-ments in recent years, such as the revolutions in information technology by computers and word processors, in transport, in telecommunications and so on, should direct us to a more accurate understanding of economic systems. That is, we should see such progress as a consequence of individuals making *speculative* leaps in a world of uncertainty rather than adjusting their actions to some hypothetical equilibrium: a phenomenon that exists only in the textbooks written by mathematical economists. Although such 'speculative leaps' are not formally incompatible with Hahnian sequential economics, there may be better and very different ways of understanding them. Schumpeter's notion of the entrepreneur as a 'creative innovator' may be one. In his theory the entrepreneur plays a disequilibriating role, upsetting a previously stable state of affairs by introducing a new product or applying a new technology.[3]

As the late Alan Coddington pointed out,[4] Hahn is wedded to the formal deductive method in economy theory, a method that sacrifices descriptive realism for logical rigour. It is impossible to capture by abstract axiomatic reasoning the real work of the

1 F. A. Hayek, *Individualism and Economic Order*, Routledge & Kegan Paul, London, 1948.

2 'The Winter of Our Discontent', *op. cit.*, p. 324 (italics added).

3 J. Schumpeter, *Capitalism, Socialism and Democracy*, Allen & Unwin, London, 1940.

4 A. Coddington, 'The Rationale of General Equilibrium Theory', *Economic Inquiry*, 13 (1975), p. 547.

Invisible Hand, which is done in the co-ordinating processes of the market. Hahn shows some recognition of this criticism when he concedes that 'general equilibrium is strong on equilibrium but very weak on how it comes about'.[1] That is, it indicates the end-state without explaining how the economy reaches it. It is not at all clear, however, that a continual refinement of the equilibrium theory is likely to be successful in answering his own pertinent question on how equilibrium is created.

What is worse, Hahn uses theory in a systematically misleading manner. Although he concedes that general equilibrium is a self-contained (mathematical) exercise that does not picture reality, he uses it to 'falsify' the major claim of the Invisible Hand theory: that an unhampered, decentralised market economy will tend to produce a situation in which no further change can be made without making at least one person worse off. (This is known as the Pareto-optimum, named after the Italian economist.) Hahn does this by showing that, in comparison with the perfect co-ordination of plans described by pure theory, existing markets display many 'inefficiencies' that could in theory be eliminated. This argument, however, is misleading; general equilibrium theory is not a causal explanation of how markets work but a self-contained logical exercise that deliberately excludes the co-ordinating processes of the real world.

Implicit theory of normative economics

Implicit also in this type of analysis is a theory of normative economics—of what policy 'ought' to be followed. What Hahn wants to show is that in a variety of areas the (alleged) failures of the market—in terms of the standards set by abstract theory—can be corrected by government and administrative action, presumably informed by the equations of general equilibrium theory. But there are, of course, government failures, which some economists forget or ignore, as well as market failures: and nothing in the general equilibrium theory allows us to compare them in terms of the magnitude of their effects on welfare. On the problems of exhaustible resources, externalities and public goods and so on, there is, in Coddington's words, still the 'possibility that the imperfectly-functioning markets perform better than any of the available (administrative) alternatives'[2]

---

[1] 'The Winter of Our Discontent', p. 327.

[2] Coddington, 'The Rationale of General Equilibrium Theory', *op. cit.*, p. 554.

(including, we must add, the usual resort to government intervention).

Thus even though the newer version of Hahnian equilibrium includes some subjectivist elements of reaction to events, it no more captures the essence of the Invisible Hand theory than does the static model he is so anxious to refine. He has not produced an account of its movement at all, but engineered a sophisticated sleight of hand. His sequential equilibrium is still a description of the *outcome* of a market process and not an account of the *process* itself. Hahn has postulated an economic 'end-state' after the Invisible Hand has done its work, but he has not revealed how this work is done.

Although no specific policy conclusions follow from general equilibrium theory—it is, in its purest form, an extraordinarily abstract theory—other (less reticent) political economists have used the ideal of an equilibrium end-state as a normative criterion (of what should be done) to attack the performance of existing capitalist economies. This style of economic reasoning is especially true of market socialists (below, pp. 58-59).

Assumptions about human behaviour

Yet if these end-state models of general equilibrium are to be put to practical political use, three assumptions about human nature are required. First, and most important of all, is the knowledge of tastes, prices and costs that would be required if the perfect equilibrium is to be *commanded* (that it can be commanded is implicit in some equilibrium models). Since those data can be revealed only by a market *process*, through entrepreneurial trial and error, any attenuation of that process simply disrupts the flow of knowledge on which economic decision-making depends. Secondly, it presupposes that economic (and, indeed, social) order is the product of someone's deliberate design and intention, but experience of the real world shows that those regularities in social affairs which have any claim to be scientific 'laws' are the *unintended* consequences of human action (below, pp. 44-48). Thirdly, and especially damaging, the model proposes no theory which can explain the behaviour of *government*: it is simply assumed to be an omniscient and benevolent agent. Yet it must come from political processes, and there can be no guarantee that such processes, democratic or otherwise, will generate such an entity. Least of all can we assume that such entities are benevolent—immune from the egoistic motivations that are operative even in Hahnian markets.

In practice, the mathematical-equilibrium economists do not use their models of the economy in this way. It would be quite wrong to accuse Hahn of making these assumptions. The equilibrium 'state of affairs' that he attempts to explain (and 'objectify') is an unintended outcome of the actions of economic agents; and his methodology is rigorously individualistic. I doubt very much whether he would have any sympathy with the way the equilibrium approach has been used by some writers, such as the market socialists, Oskar Lange and Abba Lerner (below, pp. 58-59). Yet it seems to me important to contrast his explanation of an economy with others, such as process theories, which have an equal claim to a proper understanding of market behaviour.

B. The Doctrine of Utilitarianism

My second example of an end-state theory, an approach that envisages and explains an ideal state, is drawn from the history of political thought. Although it is perhaps less sophisticated than the previous example and more overtly normative, it exhibits similar structural features. This is utilitarianism. Although the type associated with Jeremy Bentham and his followers comes from the 19th century, it is still relevant to contemporary public policy debates.

In a much more obvious and striking way than equilibrium economics, utilitarian ethics and politics presupposes that social well-being is very much a product of *deliberate* government action.

The doctrine proposes that we can evaluate societies 'scientifically', by comparing various end-states, in terms of (hypothetically) measurable utility. It is a 'welfarist' doctrine in which alternative policies are evaluated by their capacity to create social welfare, in terms of the desirable consequences (measured in benefits or pleasure) they produce. It has a connection, although tenuous, with individualism insofar that a social utility function, a summing up of total utility, is somehow computed from individual utilities. A simple example is the utilitarian theory of punishment. A wrong-doer is punished not because he *deserves* punishment for the 'wrongness' of his action but because the prospect of pain will be sufficient to deter him and others from committing harmful acts, so producing a net benefit to society as a whole.

Put this way, utilitarianism has always been vulnerable to the charge that the injunction merely to maximise social utility obliterates the *distributive* question of *who* is to be the recipient of pleasures and pains. If the end-state is the highest total utility, does its distribution to individuals matter? If the object is to diminish national crime or prevent social disorder, would not that policy license the punishment of the innocent or detention without trial if it could be shown that these punishments were effective, irrespective of the resulting violation of individual rights? Utilitarians have answers to those questions but I raise them largely to anticipate differences between utilitarianism and liberalism, which in contrast is a doctrine pre-eminently concerned with the moral claim that we should respect persons as ends in themselves, and not merely as units in an aggregate social welfare function. In other words, they should not be used as a means to the realisation of collective end-states.

Bentham's 'felicific calculus'

In its original formulation by Jeremy Bentham in the early 19th century, the end-state towards which utilitarian legislation should be directed—'the greatest happiness of the greatest number'—was computed in terms of an objective measure: units of pleasure. Although a present-day utilitarian is unlikely to believe in what is called Bentham's 'felicific calculus', he will still want to rank alternative end-states in terms of beneficial social consequences—even if they are calibrated in other than directly measurable pleasures.

In its extreme form—'act-utilitarianism'—a legislator is licensed to act in any way that would advance the well-being of the community *taken as a whole*. This proposition is axiomatically end-state. Rules and procedures are merely provisional, to be discarded if it can be shown that, in so doing, the public good would be advanced. Following rules for which there is no *immediate* rational justification is regarded as almost irrational, mystical and superstitious. It cannot be denied that many modern social policies, such as unfunded pension schemes, rent controls, and extensive 'unpriced' welfare provisions, are justified in this way: they are said to capture an immediate advantage which would not occur if individuals conducted their lives according to market principles and followed general rules.

To a social scientist who emphasises the importance of process or procedure in explaining the working of society, this approach represents all too well the hubris of reason—the arrogance and insolence of 'rational man'. It is impossible, in a necessarily uncertain world, to *know* the consequences of political (or any human) action with anything approaching certainty. Indeed, most political actions by government generate unintended consequences which are impossible to control, even if they can be predicted.

Two obvious examples here are reflation to cure unemployment and easily obtainable, universal state welfare. The *direct* implementation of a utilitarian end-state presupposes two characteristics: omniscience on the part of the legislator in knowing the consequences of political acts, as well as benevolence in wanting to perform beneficial acts. In the absence of this omniscience, the likely consequence (*sic*) of act-utilitarianism is the continual re-writing of the details of the end-state in response to the necessarily changing facts and circumstances of a complex society. Yet such frenetic revision of end-states that inevitably accompanies act-utilitarianism generates *unpredictability* for the participants in a social system. The conduct of post-war British economic policy on unemployment and inflation under the auspices of J. M. Keynes, this century's most brilliant act-utilitarian, may be taken as the most striking example of this approach.

Keynesian macro-economic 'act-utilitarianism'

In Keynesian macro-economics, policy is directed towards the *immediate* solution of a problem (unemployment) and little or no attention is paid to the possibly malign long-term consequences of the solution. This is why Keynes opposed binding monetary and constitutional rules: these were regarded as archaic impediments to the implementation of 'rational' policies. Yet predictability can be guaranteed only by rules that are more or less stable and permanent. And to be predictable, rules cannot be provisional.

Why there is a tendency for intellectuals, in this century, to take the short-run view of the effects of their proposed economic policies is difficult to say. The economic theory of democracy, developed by the economists who analyse 'public choice', has a plausible explanation. It postulates that the process of electoral competition has a tendency to shorten the time-horizons of politicians. It is a convincing explanation of the behaviour of post-war democratic governments in the West and something that Keynes himself failed to anticipate, partly because he acted on it himself, as revealed in his reaction to Hayek that if his policies produced inflation, he would change public opinion.[1]

A further sceptical observation about end-state act-utilitarianism relates to its account of the moral status of the individual. Although it is claimed that utilitarianism constructs its end-state from the preference orderings of individuals, its conception of the individual is curiously attenuated, narrow and parsimonious. The individual is not conceived as an end in himself, but merely as the carrier of utility: as long as total utility is maximised no further questions need to be asked about the ends and purposes of the people who are to experience it, or the distribution of utility between them. The economist Amartya Sen of Harvard and the philosopher Bernard Williams, now at Berkeley, write: 'persons do not count as individuals in this any more than individual petrol tanks do in the analysis of the national consumption of petroleum'.[2] An individual is thus the bearer of utilities, not of moral and economic rights, and conflicts can arise between the demands of utility-maximisation and the claims of rights. That is what is meant by the claim of the philosopher John Rawls that utilitarianism destroys the 'separateness' of persons.[3]

The inequality of utilitarianism

To the familiar charge that utilitarianism sanctions a grossly inegalitarian distribution of wealth, income and opportunities so long as *total* utility is maximised (the pleasures of the rich are supposed to outweigh the deprivations of the poor), many present-day utilitarians have an equally familiar answer. They assume that the utility of 'marginal' additions of income is the same for all individuals, so that re-distribution of income towards equality maximises total utility because the re-distribution hurts the rich *less* than it benefits the poor. The headlong rush towards

[1] IEA Video, *John Maynard Keynes: Life, Ideas, Legacy*, written and presented by Mark Blaug, Diverse Production for the IEA, 1988 (distributed by Guild Sound and Vision Ltd., Peterborough).

[2] A. Sen and B. Williams (eds.), *Utilitarianism and Beyond*, Cambridge University Press, Cambridge, 1982, p. 4.

[3] J. Rawls, *A Theory of Justice*, Clarendon Press, Oxford, 1972, pp. 22-27.

complete equality is slowed down only by the further utilitarian consideration of the disincentive effect such a policy may have on production. This was the way that the English economist Francis Edgeworth in the last century tried to justify scientifically progressive income tax without an appeal to moral concepts of equality and social justice. But the manoeuvre depends upon an interpersonal comparison of utilities. In its absence people are being used as means to the ends of the fictitious entity of 'society' implied in the notion of maximising total utility as measured in a social welfare function.

Although this doctrine is frequently exploited by egalitarians, there is no logical necessity for it to be used in this way. For if, by an interpersonal comparison of utility, it could be shown that the rich experience great pleasure from a re-distribution of income to them from the poor, total utility would be increased by inegalitarian tax policies![1]

Nevertheless, no procedural theorist who emphasises market process can entirely reject the claims of utilitarianism. For, as I shall show (below, pp. 54-56), he will want to claim some considerable consequentialist, or *indirect*,[2] utilitarian value for those rules and procedures which, he says, make regularity and predictability possible. Yet such value cannot be directly calculated by an omniscient mind; it must be a product of experience or tradition. And the 'hardness' or durability of rules is attested to by the approbation of many minds.

C. THE END-GOAL OF SOCIAL JUSTICE

My third example of an end-state approach is the strongly urged contemporary demand that an economic 'end-state' should reflect the principles of 'social' justice. It is maintained that the distribution of income and wealth in a community should not be determined by the 'random' or blind forces of the market but by 'rational' moral principles. The unpredictable and often fortuitous outcomes of the market should be controlled and corrected by values embodied in a more ethically pleasing end-state.

[1] A critique of this whole approach is in Martin Ricketts, 'Tax Theory and Tax Policy', in A. Peacock and F. Forte (eds.), *The Political Economy of Taxation*, Basil Blackwell, Oxford, 1981, pp. 29-46.

[2] John Gray, 'Indirect Utility and Fundamental Rights', in Ellen Frankel Paul and Jeffrey Paul (eds.), *Human Rights*, Blackwell, Oxford, 1984, pp. 73-91.

Income should reflect desert, merit and 'need' rather than the *value* of labour services as revealed in market exchange.

The underlying rationale of this theory depends on the distinction between the laws of production and of distribution, first urged by John Stuart Mill in his *Principles of Political Economy* (1848). At its crudest, it implies that payment can be made to individuals irrespective of the goods and services they produce: that the social cake can be sliced up in any way we like without there being any 'feed-back' on the way the cake is baked or on its quality or size.

Efficiency or social justice?

Such a distinction is untenable. The 'distributive earnings' of the factors of production, wages to labour, interest on capital and rent to land, are the necessary inducements required to draw them into production. To alter the 'outcome' of an economic system, the output of goods and services, by reference to the external principles of social justice is to alter the productive process itself. Thus to pay labour of any kind less than its marginal product is to cause a misallocation of resources: in a word, *inefficiency*. The end-state theorist is then left with an unappetising choice: efficiency or social justice? In the absence of any procedure for judging the validity of outcomes we cannot know which is preferable.

Incidentally, little of this argument affects the potency of a subtly different doctrine of social justice, to which the adjective 'social' may not be entirely appropriate. It concentrates less on the 'justice' of the outcome of a productive process and much more on the starting point. It is the distribution of initial resources that may be called 'unjust', not the result of the 'game' itself. It may be possible, therefore, to alter the array of property holdings in economic society without having quite the un-intended effect on efficiency alluded to above. The ownership of a non-augmentable resource used in production, particularly land, is an important example. For it is a logical truth that an exchange process must begin with objects which are themselves not the product of exchange. Before something can be exchanged for something else, it must already be 'owned'. How things come to be owned is not an issue that concerns orthodox economists because it involves key *moral* questions of legitimacy and entitlement (below, pp. 64-66).

[42]

Summary

The defining characteristics of political end-state theories may now be briefly summarised. First, they attribute the production of desirable outcomes to *intentional* acts of individuals (or bodies). Second, they emphasise the role of an active *reason* in the determination of social events. Third, they depend heavily on the centralisation of knowledge. Fourth, they depend ultimately on the existence of benevolent and omniscient dictators. Social process theories may be understood as responses to all of these assumptions; they are better efforts to explain the working of politico-economic society because they avoid the objections and weaknesses of end-state theories.

III. SELF-GENERATING AND SELF-CORRECTING
SOCIAL PROCESSES

I have distinguished three examples of end-states in economic and social theory: not all of them are mutually consistent. But all process theories in principle have a common element: they explain a social and economic order in terms of its self-generating and self-correcting properties.

To understand a social system in terms of process and procedure is not in itself to commit the social theorist to any particular political position. Nevertheless, the connection between process theory and liberal-individualist political economy is not coincidental. There are good reasons why it should hold. Marxism is a version of a process methodology since it is a dynamic theory that stresses the mechanisms of social and economic change. Yet, since it understands social laws in terms of historical categories, such as 'classes', rather than as inferences from universally true features of the human condition, it does not fit into the type I am discussing here.

Unintended consequences – the evolutionary process

The defining feature of social process theories is that they interpret regularities as the unintended consequences of human action and not as the deliberate intentions of individuals. They constitute a most striking contrast with conspiracy theories of history. The idea that there can be order and regularity without design, and that social change can be explained without recourse to deliberate human actions, was discovered by the thinkers of the 18th-century Scottish Enlightenment, notably Adam Ferguson, David Hume and Adam Smith, long before Darwin in a not dissimilar way explained the biological world without the intervention of a Creator. The point was put beautifully by Ferguson in 1767:

> 'Every step and every movement of the multitude, even in what are termed enlightened ages are made with equal blindness to the future; and nations stumble upon establishments, which are indeed the result of human action, but not the execution of any human design.'[1]

[1] A. Ferguson, *An Essay on Civil Society*, ed. by Duncan Forbes, Edinburgh University Press, Edinburgh, 1966.

What Ferguson had in mind was the emergence, by an evolutionary process, of such phenomena as the co-ordinating properties of the market, the system of the Common Law, the institution of money, constitutional law, and human language itself.

The idea was taken up much later, in 1883, by the Austrian economist, Carl Menger, in his methodological work, *Problems in Sociology and Economics*. This was written as a contribution to the *Methodenstreit* (dispute over methodology) that Menger had with the German Historical School, which maintained that economics should be limited to the description of distinct social categories, such as 'feudalism' and 'capitalism', rather than concern itself with the construction of universal laws of human behaviour. Menger distinguished between *organic* institutions (which emerged in a spontaneous manner) and *pragmatic* institutions (which were a direct product of man's will). Of the former he wrote:

> 'Language, religion, law, even the state itself, and to mention a few economic and social phenomena of markets, of competition and money, and numerous other social structures are already met within epochs of history where we cannot properly speak of purposeful activity of the community as such directed at establishing them.'[1]

What Menger had in mind, of course, was the indirect utilitarian advantage to be had in relying on spontaneous forces.

This is what is meant by Invisible Hand explanations. The regularities displayed by complex phenomena, such as markets and legal orders, come about not through anyone's direct intention but as the unintended consequences of the actions of *many* men. They constitute what are know as 'third world' phenomena:[2] logically different from the *natural* phenomena of the physical world (explained by laws that operate independently of men's wills) and merely *conventional* phenomena which are directly alterable by men's wills (such as a parliamentary statute or the details of an economic plan). All that an Invisible Hand explanation claims is that there can be order without design. It is in this characteristic of human behaviour that Hayek has made his most significant contribution to the philosophy of economic and social science.

[1] C. Menger, *Problems of Economics and Sociology*, ed. by Louis Schneider, University of Illinois Press, Urbana, 1966, p. 146.

[2] Edna Ullmann-Margalit, 'Invisible Hand Explanations', *Synthese*, 30 (1979), pp. 263-81.

Anti-rationalist generation of institutions

It is, of course, true that such institutions as money and law can be, and are, deliberately produced by centralised bodies, such as central banks and parliaments; but in process explanation they are generated anyway by the actions of decentralised agents. The explanation is therefore anti-rationalist in the sense that large-scale complex phenomena that display regularities can be explained as something other than the product of an unaided human reason. To the modern rationalist it seems incredible that such complex phenomena could occur independently of human intervention. Yet, there was *law* before there was the modern, organised state; for example, the rules of property, contract and tort were developed independently of statute.

It is also true that aggregative social phenomena which display regularities may not be as beneficial (in an indirect utilitarian sense) as a market system and a Common Law process are. Indeed the British welfare state, much criticised from a free market point of view, may be said to have developed in a series of discrete steps without anybody intending the final outcome. And, of course, market systems produce 'prisoners' dilemmas', situations in which rational self-interested action leads to collectively undesirable outcomes such as pollution of the atmosphere, despoliation of the natural environment, and so on. Most Invisible Hand theorists, of course, do not deny that its movements have to be supplemented on these occasions by some form of collective action. What is denied is that there is some 'objective' solution, or efficient end-state, which government is competent to impose on inter-acting individuals. Thus the emergence of a well-ordered aggregate social and economic structure can be evaluated. Nevertheless, it must be conceded that this is a difficult problem for the proponents of the Invisible Hand theory because they wish to avoid an evaluation in accordance with some 'rational', abstract end-state. It is for this reason that a prevalent tendency among market-oriented social scientists is to seek improvements in the mechanisms of individual exchange which could eliminate the 'blockages' rather than directly try to calculate some optimum. Many of these impediments are the direct product of government itself. The most common example is rent control, which prevents mutually satisfactory exchanges between landlords and potential tenants.

Hayek has suggested, somewhat more ambitiously, that the process of evolution (not quite the same as 'Social Darwinism')

will 'select out' those aggregate structures that are more successful in meeting man's needs. Most writers have found this
implausible and indeed the historical evidence hardly points to
an ultimate triumph of the market order. However, the recent
adoption of a more favourable attitude towards the market
mechanism in Marxist régimes precisely because of its success is
perhaps an implicit acknowledgement of the evolutionary
argument. But the evidence for Hayek's solution is rather
meagre and hardly sufficient to establish it as even the beginning
of a genuine theory.

Anti-rationalist, not irrationalist

It should be emphasised, of course, that nothing in these
Invisible Hand explanations rests on the intervention of some
extra-terrestrial force (God or fate): to be an anti-rationalist is not
to be irrationalist. As David Hume said, the point of the anti-
rationalist enterprise is to use reason to 'whittle down the claims
of reason'. An example of the instrumental value of anti-
rationalist explanations is monetary regularity and stability. It
seems absurd to the modern rationalist that the money good has
to be produced by 'wasting' factors of production in digging gold
out of the ground. Yet can it really be maintained that the
rationalist invention of fiduciary money, or 'paper' backed by no
commodity, has been more successful in producing monetary
regularity and predictability than that system (the Gold
Standard) which ignorant men stumbled upon accidentally? The
inflations of the 20th century that have produced revolutions and
the destruction of social order can be traced to the breaking of
the link between the currency and a (precious) commodity that
sustained its value.

The modern development of these 18th-century ideas is in the
direction of epistemology: towards a specifically anti-rationalist
theory of knowledge. It is the theory that the kind of knowledge
(or information) that we can have of social affairs—economic,
political and legal knowledge—exists in a dispersed and fragmented form across millions of participants in a social process
and cannot be centralised or stated in the form of simple
propositions. Such knowledge is ever-changing and rarely repli-
cates itself like some ordered genetic pattern: the way that prices
constantly change in the market according to changes in tastes
and technology is a spectacular example of this process. Again,

[47]

in the language of modern philosophy, much of our knowledge consists in knowing 'how' (how to do things) rather than in knowing 'that' (knowing some more or less unchanging body of information).

Michael Polanyi (1891-1976), a modern polymath who effortlessly spanned the disciplines of chemistry, philosophy, politics, sociology and economics, made a crucial distinction between *articulated* and *tacit* knowledge in order to demonstrate that the sum of human knowledge is not exhausted by that which can be stated explicitly. Polanyi in 1959 claimed that knowledge

> 'as set out in written words, or mathematical formulae, is only one kind of knowledge; while unformulated knowledge, such as we have of something we are in fact doing, is another form of knowledge.'[1]

In other words, we always 'know more than we can tell'. The relevance of all this to the process/end-state distinction should now be clear. For, in an indirect utilitarian sense, decentralised human action, powered by self-interest and subject to constraints, will make better use of this fragmented knowledge than can centralised agencies. This view is amplified below (pp. 49-51).

---

[1] M. Polanyi, *The Study of Man*, University of Chicago Press, Chicago, 1959, p. 59.

IV. THE INVISIBLE HAND AS
AN ECONOMIC PROCESS

Perhaps the most effective argument for spontaneous forces derives from the explanation of the functioning of an economic system. The end-state described by equilibrium theory, although couched in the language of competition and markets, can be described only with full information of consumer tastes, costs, and so on. Yet there is no theory of *how* the necessary information is co-ordinated and transmitted.

The notion of the Invisible Hand must be seen as a metaphor that illuminates a continuing process of exchange and competition between individuals which brings about a co-ordination of plans and purposes. It is not a picture of an end-state of perfect equilibrium in which all plans have been 'meshed', since that implies the cessation of human action. The Invisible Hand image refers to an *unending* process of change and adjustment and not to a perfectly harmonious end-state in which incentives to change have been removed. It is because we cannot know in advance of a market process the details of the price structure of an economy in perfect equilibrium that the description of a market economy as tending to an equilibrium is misleading. The market process equilibrium is a theoretical abstraction that has no necessary connection with real markets at a point in time or over a period.

Of all the differences that mark off abstract equilibrium models from existing markets it is the omnipresence of ignorance and uncertainty that is most germane to real markets. Because market transactors, entrepreneurs, are necessarily ignorant of most of the information on the economic universe, all their actions are speculative; they have to make guesses about a necessarily unknowable future. It follows that they cannot be passive 'reactors' responding automatically to a given set of data; they are active makers of various futures. Economic activity consists of continually 'exploiting' the price differences that exist in a necessarily imperfect world. It is this, of course, that constitutes 'profit', a phenomenon which is absent from an equilibrium world. Yet if there were no possibility of profit there would be nothing to drive the system towards equilibrium. In Hayek's instructive phrase, the market is a 'discovery procedure' by which transactors adjust themselves to ever-changing circumstances, rather than an 'allocative device' by which means are somehow mechanistically directed to the production of given ends. Entrepreneurs are thus essentially the co-ordinators of the tacit knowledge that exists in human society.

We can now see how genuine market competition differs from the ersatz version described in the 'perfectly competitive equilibrium' models still reproduced in textbooks. As the Chicago economist Frank Knight said, 'in perfect competition there is no competition'. If there are no mistaken prices to correct, as in perfect competition, there is no opportunity for the intense rivalry that characterises economic action to manifest itself and no necessity for entrepreneurship to play its co-ordinating role.

The failure of planning (UK) . . .

Perhaps the only examples in British history (outside wartime) of government attempting to 'manage' an economy independently of (or in defiance of) spontaneous processes were the 1945-51 and 1964-70 Labour Governments, echoed by the Conservatives in the early 1960s and early 1970s. In these periods rationing, controls over production and incomes, and the setting of national targets constituted a method or plan which was designed to produce an outcome superior to that which would have resulted from the apparently unco-ordinated actions of decentralised agents. Yet, as recorded in John Jewkes' neglected book, *Ordeal by Planning*, that era was characterised by unprecedented (in peace-time) shortages and economic dislocation. Despite possessing an immense array of economic statistics and other 'data', government found itself responding to events rather than determining them: a grim tribute to the flux and uncertainty of economic society. In Jewkes' words: 'each new plan was clearly obsolete, over-run by the speed of events as soon as published'.[1] The most spectacular example was the fuel crisis of 1947, which occurred precisely because of the Government's refusal to let the price mechanism allocate resources.

---

[1] J. Jewkes, *The New Ordeal by Planning*, Macmillan, London, 1968, p. 95; this was the second edition of Jewkes' *Ordeal by Planning* (first published in 1948).

... and the success of social market economy (W. Germany)

What is surprising about economic commentary in the last thirty years, both academic and popular, is the neglect of the experience of the West German Social Market Economy, inaugurated in 1950 by Ludwig Erhard. Only recently has it been noted that German economic recovery came about through the application of market principles.[1] From 1933 onwards the German economy under Hitler had been subjected to an unprecedented amount of controls and regulations—which persisted during the period of Allied occupation. By 1950 it was still in a ruinous state, not merely because of Germany's defeat. Yet with the lifting of almost all the controls the West German economy recovered rapidly; by the end of the 1950s it was at the top of the European economic league. What is intriguing about this example is that Germany's historical and intellectual traditions (in economics and sociology) were unfavourable to markets. As has been often said, there was no German 'miracle' but rather the unsurprising results of the application of a well-founded theory.

'Human action, not human design'

In economics the purpose of the Invisible Hand theory is to show how there can be order without a designing mind and without anyone intending specifically to produce such an order. Hayek's famous observation, echoing Ferguson in 1767, that the social sciences should be concerned with the investigation of phenomena that are 'the result of human action, but not of human design' shows that there are 'natural' processes at work that, if left undisturbed, will produce an order infinitely more subtle and complex than that which emanates from deliberate human will. The reason for its superiority is essentially that no one mind can have access to the widely dispersed knowledge which is a feature of a natural system. To think that this access is possible is, according to Hayek, to be a victim of the 'synoptic delusion'. As he has systematically emphasised, a self-correcting economic system is not the only example of a natural social process; legal systems and languages, for example, display similar properties.

Professor Sen thinks that this is rather an 'unprofound' thought.[2] He supports this contention by giving a trivial example

---

[1] K. Zweig, *The Origins of the Social Market Economy in Germany*, Adam Smith Institute, London, 1980.

[2] A. K. Sen, 'The Profit Motive', *Lloyds Bank Review*, January 1983, p. 3.

of an action—crossing the street—from which certain results occurred that were not specifically designed; for example, crossing the street led to a passing car being delayed. This illustration is disingenuous, for the fascinating truth about Invisible Hand theories is that they produce surprising and *untrivial* results. *The typical modern intellectual is a victim of the synoptic delusion.* It is inconceivable to him that a market can co-ordinate human relationships in the absence of a central human agency: yet all of the movements towards economic planning in Britain, from the 1961 growth targets set by NEDC, through the 1965 'National Plan' of George Brown, to the 'National Economic Assessment' suggested by Labour at the 1987 General Election, are based on the dubious claim that a handful of politicians and their advisers can know more than the myriad of individuals in the market. It is also difficult for the present-day social scientist to concede that judges evolving Common Law in a case-by-case manner can generate a more predictable legal order than that produced by legislatures creating statute law. Yet it is these private processes in markets and Common Law systems that are orderly; and it is the human will re-inforced by the power to coerce that is capricious.

The claim that the Common Law system is an aggregate structure of rules, the entirety of which no one person designed, and that it effectively co-ordinates the actions of decentralised agents successfully does not imply that it is 'efficient' in some perfectionist or 'optimal' sense (although some economists have implied that this is, indeed, its rationale). But, for example, the evolution of the law of torts has enabled individuals to sue for recoverable damages when harms have been inflicted upon them. It has provided both the deterrence effect in discouraging individuals from actions that reduce others' welfare and the compensation effect of restoring individuals to their position before the harm. It may not be perfectly efficient since costs in money and time involved in legal action sometimes mean that remedies are not adequately provided so that an 'optimum' allocation of resources is not achieved. But the significant comparison should be with *public* and statutory law rather than with an imaginary optimum. For 'made' or enacted law in these activities often has the effect of reducing 'economising' action by the people engaged in them since it removes personal liability from individuals for the harms they cause. An example is the establishment of 'no fault' accident laws, in New Zealand and elsewhere, which, it is estimated, have led to a 10-15 per cent *increase* in accidents.[1]

Common law v. statute law

The comparison between common and statute law is not necessarily clarified by empirical data alone—who can say which is the more 'efficient'? There are really two types of legal 'order', that brought about by design and that which emerges in a spontaneous manner. A difficulty with designed orders is that they depend very much on the caprice of legislatures, bodies that are often dictated to by pressure groups, and their behaviour may be much less predictable than the abstract and impersonal rules of the Common Law. All too often the assumption is made by rationalists that without specific legislative intervention there would be widespread disco-ordination in these areas. Indeed, one of the most damaging pieces of statute law in Britain this century was the 1906 Trade Disputes Act which made trade unions immune from tort actions arising out of industrial dispute. Such a privilege could never have emerged from the Common Law: yet it is statutory legal phenomena such as this that have done so much to create disharmony in industrial relations and disco-ordination in the market.

The most that Professor Sen concedes is that the market is appropriate (only) for those matters over which people's interests converge. But he maintains that it is quite irrelevant for those activities where there is a conflict of interests. In one sense he is uttering a tautology: market relationships *are* convergent ones and, where there are irreconcilable conflicts, trading is impossible. The important feature about the familiar institutions of market society is that they enable individuals to discover those areas where co-operation and gains from trade are possible. We cannot know what co-ordination can take place until we allow people to exercise their 'natural propensity to truck, barter and exchange', as Adam Smith put it in a famous phrase. The danger of over-emphasising the conflictual side of human relationships is that it licenses 'politics' to dominate men's lives, and politics has an almost irreversible tendency to conceal the opportunities for agreement among people. The whole question of the role of politics in economic and social life will be considered below (pp. 75-83).

[1] E. M. Landes, 'Insurance, Liability and Accidents: a theoretical and empirical investigation of the effect of no-fault on accidents', *Journal of Law & Economics*, 25 (1982), pp. 49-65.

V. THE SELF-CORRECTING PROCESS

We are now in a better position to scrutinise more critically the normative implication that lurks in the complexity of the conventional version of the Invisible Hand theory. The obvious imperfections, such as monopoly power, of real-world markets are emphasised by critics of the market as departures from some imaginary social optimum crying out for governmental correction. But if no social optimum exists independently of the actions of economic transactors, how can there be an infallible touchstone that measures so exquisitely all of our economic variables? The familiar market imperfections, since they represent opportunities for speculative gain, are themselves being constantly corrected by enterprising individuals through the market process. If there is nothing in economic behaviour apart from the actions of individuals, from where do we derive an instrument for calibrating those actions? From which source does the state derive the knowledge necessary for co-ordination?

It follows that there are two problems for the general equilibrium versions of the Invisible Hand theorem. First, there is the epistemological argument that the nature of free economic activity, which is essentially unpredictable, precludes any observer having the *knowledge* required to make any statement about a social optimum meaningful. Second, even if the idea of such an optimum could be made operational, how would we guarantee that government action would produce it more effectively than private agents? Why should political officials be more informed about profitable opportunities than market traders who risk their own resources? Furthermore, as the public-choice school of political economy[1] has shown, we cannot be at all confident that political officials will maximise such social optima in the absence of strict constitutional rules. In the real world of party politics and bureaucracy, the reverse is likely: officials will maximise their private interests. Moreover, if authoritarianism is to be avoided in the management of the

---

[1] An accessible introduction to public choice theory is in G. Tullock, *The Vote Motive*, Hobart Paperback 9, IEA, 1976. A more advanced treatment is in D. Mueller, *Public Choice*, Cambridge University Press, Cambridge, 1979.

economy, organised groups, such as trade unions and business organisations, will have to be involved in the decision-making process. The natural tendency of these bodies is to advance their sectional interests. A market is essentially a process that is in the long-term interests of anonymous individuals rather than in their short-term interests as members of politically active groups.

Time, the market and the Invisible Hand

The market is a process that operates through time; it is not characterised by the instantaneous adjustment of carefully programmed automatons. If the Invisible Hand's operation were as described in the general equilibrium theory, there would be no need for money, the firm, entrepreneurship and all the other economic categories that exist because of the ineradicable uncertainty that pervades economic life in the real world. The interesting question concerns not the existence of perfect co-ordination in the unreal world of abstract equilibrium, but the nature of the co-ordinating process the Invisible Hand generates in the world we know.

Here there would appear to be some disagreement between the various anti-equilibrium schools of political economy. The Austrian tradition, as exemplified by Mises and Hayek, holds that there is a tendency to equilibrium: it does not consist of an instantaneous price and quantity adjustment, but of a learning process in which individual plans are co-ordinated. A more extreme subjectivist position, associated mainly with the work of G. L. S. Shackle,[1] holds that, because economic life consists entirely of thoughts and expectations about the future which may turn out to be wrong, one cannot even posit a tendency to equilibrium. The world is 'kaleidic' rather than smoothly co-ordinating, and the entrepreneur is a creative innovator rather than an agent who merely brings about an alignment of dispersed information.

The alleged failure of the Invisible Hand derives not from the unreal and mechanistic approaches advanced by Professors Hahn and Sen, but from a subtle interpretation of the very process that their analytical 'models' conceal. However, irrespective of the subtleties of Shackle's argument, historical experience suggests that the disruptions to the co-ordinating process that do occur come from government intervention rather than

---

[1] G. L. S. Shackle, *Epistemics and Economics*, Cambridge University Press, Cambridge, 1976.

from organic internal features of the market exchange system. Throughout the 20th century, government mismanagement of money has had catastrophic disco-ordinating effects on unemployment and inflation. The plethora of welfare, housing and trade union legislation has systematically rendered large parts of the labour force virtually immobile. In other words, the Invisible Hand is not naturally or incurably arthritic: it has impediments artificially imposed by government actions that cramp its movements.

When the market is understood as a co-ordinating device we can see how it is constantly correcting those 'inefficiencies' of an economic system which are revealed when the end-state equilibrium theorist 'freezes frame' on the video film of society. Monopolies and other market imperfections are constantly, though not instantaneously, being corrected by competitive processes. Furthermore, the problem of the 'detrimental externalities' that the end-state theorists noticed may well be soluble within process theory itself for, if left alone, the Common Law, made by judges in the light of individual cases, itself generates new rules to deal with unexpected circumstances. The questions raised by damage to the environment caused by pollution are answerable within a legal framework that specifies property rights. The process theory holds that centralised administration is ill-equipped to handle such problems precisely because it possesses only *articulated* knowledge, while an Invisible Hand process generates and co-ordinates *tacit* knowledge.

Pigou, Coase and social cost

One of the most important developments in spontaneous order theory is the application of standard economic reasoning to problems of the environment: especially those cases where the actions of a producer using the least-cost methods of production impose damages on third parties. Since A. C. Pigou's pioneering work[1] in this sphere it has been assumed that such activities necessarily required corrective action by the state. Since the producer does not have to bear the cost of the damage he causes he will 'over-produce', which will be inefficient from the perspective of the community. It was assumed that social efficiency could be achieved only through public action in the form of taxation, regulation or outright nationalisation.

It has been shown, however, that in circumstances such as

[1] A. C. Pigou, *The Economics of Welfare*, Macmillan, London, 1920.

these, bargaining between the parties may produce an efficient outcome or 'internalise' the externalities. R. H. Coase (1960), in a famous article,[1] showed that whatever the distribution of legal entitlements and property rights, economic transactors would have an incentive to remove the externality through trade. Thus in his example of a train emitting sparks onto land where farmers planted seed, the parties could always reach an agreement between themselves which was mutually beneficial. If, for example, the farmers held the right of veto, the railroad company could always compensate them for damage (and *vice versa*) up to the point at which the marginal benefit equalled the marginal cost. Again, the familiar example of a factory-owner polluting a stream and therefore damaging fishing stocks can be handled in the same way. The point of Coase's analysis was to show that it is not necessarily economically efficient to impose all the costs unilaterally on the producer—which is the strong implication of the Pigovian analysis.

Coase, of course, makes some rather heroic assumptions: notably that property rights be fully specified and that transactions costs are zero. The latter assumption may look more than a little optimistic in cases of negative externality that involve large numbers of people; here the possibilities of 'free-riding' may deter people from negotiating an agreement to eliminate an external harm.

Nevertheless, the argument is an important adjunct to the Invisible Hand theory. It shows that the problem of externalities is very often a problem about the obstacles to a negotiated agreement. Attention should surely be directed to the removal of those obstacles (such as uncertainty about property rights). The Pigovian approach presupposes that government should calculate some social 'optimum' and impose it on transactors. But the assumptions here are perhaps even more heroic than those made by Coase: namely, that government can calculate exactly the appropriate tax required to unite marginal private and marginal social costs, and can be relied upon to implement it impartially. The first question is about knowledge and the second about motivation. In all such cases there are no perfect solutions. However, in a comparison between two (admittedly) imprecise instruments, the market and the state, the assumption that the state is less imperfect than the market is arbitrary.

[1] R. H. Coase, 'The Problem of Social Cost', *Journal of Law & Economics*, 3 (1960), pp. 1-44. Also S. Cheung, *The Myth of Social Cost*, Hobart Paper 82, IEA, 1978.

VI. THE ERRORS OF MARKET SOCIALISM

In recent years there has been some recognition by socialist economists and other scholars[1] of the truth that markets allocate resources more efficiently, and reflect consumer choice more faithfully, than centralised planning. There is a belated recognition that to some extent the market is a neutral instrument whose efficiency properties can be used to serve a variety of political ends. The claim is now even made that markets could work better under socialism: that the capitalist system of private ownership is itself an impediment to the full realisation of the powers of a pure exchange system.

There is nothing new about market socialism. Its most sophisticated formulation, that produced by Oskar Lange and Abba Lerner in the 1930s, was decisively refuted by Hayek (building on the earlier work of Mises).[2] The major aim of market socialism is to drive a wedge between the market and capitalism and to argue that the system can work without private property and profit.

It is apparent that market socialism is a variant of general equilibrium theory. For if an equilibrium could be replicated in the real world it would have egalitarian features. Since there is no entrepreneurship there is no profit, and the income paid to the factors of production is precisely that required to keep them in their most efficient uses. Socialists have rarely noticed that a competitive system shows a natural tendency to eliminate unproductive inequality.

But market socialism fails for exactly the same reasons as general equilibrium theory itself: because of the problems of knowledge and human motivation.

The problem of knowledge is simply that without a market process, which is inevitably a system of trial and error, information about consumer tastes and productive techniques cannot be transmitted to economic managers. Theorists of

---

[1] Ian Forbes (ed.), *Market Socialism: Whose Choice?*, Fabian Society, No. 516, London, 1986.

[2] Hayek's essays on 'Socialist Calculation', in *Individualism and Economic Order*, Routledge and Kegan Paul, London, 1948, and his most recent rejection of market socialism in 'The Impossibility of Socialist Calculation', *Economic Affairs*, April 1982.

market socialism suppose that managers can be given instructions, for example, to 'price at marginal cost'. But how can this cost be known? In market theory the cost of producing a particular good is the value of the next best alternative use of the same resources. This, of course, is a subjective judgement: it can be revealed only by genuine real-life competition between resource owners. In the absence of such a process the orders issued to economic managers are literally empty, artificial, political fabrications.

Entrepreneurial risk-taking = economic progress

Perhaps of more direct relevance is that, without the prospect of entrepreneurial gain, many risky activities would not be embarked upon. The argument that managers will be paid their marginal product, in accordance with the allocational principles of equilibrium theory, evades the problem. For such a payment is only meaningful in *repetitive* economic activity: when costs are already known and an equilibrium has been reached. But economic progress is possible only when risks are taken, and in this scenario entrepreneurial profits (and, let us not forget, losses) are inevitable. Such profits will be constantly whittled down as long as the competitive process is allowed to proceed.

It should also be emphasised that the public benefit that emerges from a competitive process that allows a free rein to entrepreneurship is an *incidental* outcome: it is neither deliberately planned nor dependent upon the goodwill of benevolent, public-spirited or 'caring' individuals. It is the *system* that generates well-being. Economic arrangements that dispense with Invisible Hand mechanisms depend ultimately on goodwill for beneficence to be produced. *Yet the familiar features of human nature are not suspended merely because the market process has been attenuated.* Entrepreneurship is still a feature of socialist economic management: but it is more likely to be reflected in political aggrandisement than in serving the interests of the consumer.

VII. THE INVISIBLE HAND, JUSTICE AND WELFARE

Although many socialist and other critics of the market concede that it is a remarkably efficient economic mechanism, the argument is often advanced that it is bought at quite a high cost. It is suggested that an unhampered market periodically produces mass unemployment, pockets of poverty amid affluence, 'externalities' in the form of pollution and other damage to the environment, and failure to generate growth in Third World countries. In all of this critique there is scarcely any recognition of the obvious truth that no other economic system has remotely approached capitalism in its productivity and ability to satisfy consumer wants, and its capacity to generate welfare.

Of these criticisms, the work of Professor Sen deserves most respect.[1] He does not deny that the market is an indispensable institution and is quick to concede that the wholesale abandonment of the exchange mechanism would produce general impoverishment. Yet he claims that we must assess its claims by reference to criteria that lie outside it: 'we have to place the role of markets in a fuller *moral* context'.[2] The criteria Professor Sen undoubtedly has in mind are justice and welfare.

What is social justice?

I have alluded earlier (pp. 41-43) to the end-state problem: should a 'socially just' outcome be preferred to an efficient allocation of resources? But there is also a difficulty about the meaning of social justice itself. Some market theorists claim that there is no reason in logic or ethics why any particular outcome, like a given distribution of income and wealth, of an Invisible Hand process should be selected and thence valued. In process theory we cannot attribute justice to *collective outcomes* at all but only to *individual action* under general rules of just conduct (of which those of the Common Law are the most familiar type). Since outcomes are the products of the *unintended* consequences of

---

[1] A. Sen, 'The Profit Motive', *op. cit.*, and 'The Moral Standing of the Market', in Ellen Frankel Paul, Fred D. Miller and Jeffrey Paul (eds.), *Ethics and Economics*, Basil Blackwell, Oxford, 1985, pp. 1-19.

[2] 'The Moral Standing of the Market', *ibid.*, p. 2 (italics added).

human action, moral concepts of approbation and disapprobation are entirely inappropriate. We can no more blame the outcomes of a process, such as the market, for its injustice than British people can blame the weather for its inequitable distribution of sunshine between these islands and Spain.

This view is perhaps an implication of only some (more extreme) versions of the Invisible Hand theory. If the theory is entirely about co-ordinating processes and is solely concerned to show that there can be an order of predictability without design, then silence about particular outcomes or states of affairs in relation to social justice would be, of course, appropriate. But in most versions of the Invisible Hand theory the claim is that spontaneous processes do, in an indirect utilitarian sense, produce more acceptable outcomes than those that could be generated artificially. No matter how reticent the evaluation of outcomes that is implied here, as a matter of logic it is an appraisal that could be extended (critically) into more overtly ethical areas. Although outcomes are not intended they are, in some circumstances, clearly *alterable*.

There are a number of possible responses to this point from the Invisible Hand theory. The argument from social justice, where it means that income distribution should be made to conform (artificially) to a pattern different from that which would emerge from free exchanges, could still be rejected without negating the case for some government intervention. One criterion, used by the German theorists of 'Social Market Economy', is *Marktkonform*. It means that a particular intervention is admissible if it conforms to the smooth operation of the price mechanism, inadmissible if it impedes it. Financial aid to the homeless is *marktkonform* because it creates markets; rent control is not because it destroys markets. Nevertheless, it has to be conceded that Invisible Hand theorists are reluctant to sanction departures from the distribution of income decreed by an unaided market either because they may have unanticipated effects on the productive process, or because they hold, in addition, some theory of inviolable property rights.

The 'catastrophic results' of unimpeded property rights (Sen)
The market system does, of course, presuppose that individuals have property rights (if they did not, what could be exchanged?). What Professor Sen has in mind is a much more serious objection: it is the possibility that catastrophic results may be a

consequence of the unimpeded exercise of those rights.[1] He maintains that they are not merely possibilities but have occurred. He cites instances of mass starvation in developing countries resulting from the perfectly proper, legal exercise of property rights. The Invisible Hand is said to fail in a welfare sense because it does not distribute food to people who need it when there is no general shortage. Thus whatever the logical objections to the moral appraisal of outcomes, Professor Sen maintains that:

> 'It is hard to imagine that the value of the market can be divorced from the value of its results and achievements'.[2]

The Invisible Hand does not merely waver, it may pack a lethal punch.

What Professor Sen has in mind are those extreme versions of the Invisible Hand theory that disallow any redistribution of property away from its rightful owners without their consent. Although there may be some truth in the claim that charitable donations may alleviate such 'catastrophes', it would be foolish to rely on this argument to counter the objections Professor Sen has raised.

These observations are mainly directed at Robert Nozick's version of the Invisible Hand theory in which the existence of rights (including legal property claims) operates as a strong side-constraint on government action.[3] In the more orthodox tradition, from Adam Smith to Friedrich Hayek, Invisible Hand processes are valued not because they are consistent with inviolable rights but because they are likely to make the best use of dispersed knowledge, and hence bring about prosperity—*at least in contrast to the known alternatives* of those that proceed by deliberate design and intention.

Thus even if perfectly legal market trading were to lead to outcomes described by Professor Sen (and their frequency may be doubted), it does not refute the argument for the Invisible Hand nor establish the case for a *dirigiste* system of production and distribution. The discovery of occasional examples of such suffering under capitalist market systems does not demonstrate that collectivism would have done any better. The more frequent cases of mass starvation under communism, as in the

---

[1] *Ibid.*, p. 5.   [2] *Ibid.*, p. 7.

[3] R. Nozick, *Anarchy, State and Utopia*, Blackwell, Oxford, 1974.

Soviet Union, Ethiopia and elsewhere, are sufficient to tip the balance in favour of *laissez-faire* even in the least propitious cases.

Professor Sen does not confine his critical observations to the developing world. He claims, in a remarkable passage, that in the market economies of the West if people do not go begging for food it is only because of the 'social security that the state has offered'.[1] Yet the high welfare payments in capitalist economies are possible only because of the surplus created by an economic system driven by the profit motive. Indeed, the social security payments in capitalist economies in many cases exceed the incomes of employed workers in planned collectivist economies of the kind preferred by critics of the market. Again, it is neither naïve nor callous to suggest that much of the unemployment that characterises market economies is a result of those very same welfare payments that cramp the movements of the Invisible Hand. People who choose subsidised leisure over paid employment are responding rationally to the signals of a distorted market. It is curious to argue that economic inefficiencies caused by state intervention that inhibits the working of the Invisible Hand constitute evidence of its failings. The very presence of extensive state welfare provisions financed by taxes on earnings from high productivity thus ironically points to the success of the profit motive.

Professor Sen might well accept some of this argument but still maintain that a market system driven purely by the profit motive could not generate the volume of welfare that some external moral criteria dictate. This retort cannot be sustained with confidence, for there is abundant historical evidence that individuals in market societies were developing extensive voluntary welfare systems, through private insurance, 'mutual aid' schemes and the like,[2] well before the development of the compulsory welfare state.

[1] Sen, 'The Profit Motive', *op. cit.*, p. 12.
[2] D. G. Green, *The Welfare State: For Rich or for Poor?*, Occasional Paper 63, IEA, London, 1982; amplified in his book, *Working Class Patients and the Medical Establishment*, Gower/Temple Smith, London, 1985.

VIII. PROPERTY AND JUSTICE

There is a general weakness in the approach of the critics of the Invisible Hand. Their obsessive concern with the alleged failures of the market process leads them to overlook the deficiencies of politics. All too often, the choice of methods is presented as if it were between the commands of a benevolent and omniscient legislator, on the one hand, and a messy and imperfect market on the other. The real comparison must, of course, be between political and economic means to generally agreed ends.

What is not often realised by critics of the Invisible Hand is that the doctrine itself is not logically the same as political liberalism, although classical liberals have made the most use of it. It is of course individualistic in the important sense that the efficiency properties of free markets are explained in terms of individual actions and volitions; but it is, nevertheless, consistent with a number of different rules of private property ownership. Since economic exchange must begin with objects and resources which *originated* by other methods than exchange, it is possible for there to be some redistribution of original resources while still permitting the market to determine future re-allocations. One of the deficiencies of Paretian welfare economics is that it is silent on the ownership system from which trading starts: it simply states that, as long as no one is made worse off by an exchange, social welfare has increased. It is true that 'unplanned' markets do bring about Pareto-improvements, but as Professor Sen rightly points out:

> 'A state in which some people are suffering from an acute depri-
> vation while others are tasting the good life can still be Pareto-
> optimal if the poor cannot be made better off without cutting into the
> pleasures of the rich'.[1]

Is there a 'just' distribution?

It may be that the catastrophies to which Professor Sen refers could have been avoided if the initial distribution of resources had been more 'just'. In many parts of the world vital resources

[1] Sen, 'The Profit Motive', *op. cit.*, p. 6.

such as land have been acquired violently by minorities rather than by the application of labour, and such acquisitions obviously have long-term implications for income and wealth distribution even under market arrangements. Invisible Hand theorists become political liberals when they produce logically independent arguments for the justification of individual acquisition of previously unowned resources, by inheritance, gifts, and other forms of entitlement. One such argument, deriving from John Locke, is that a person is entitled to that which he produces by the application of labour to a previously unowned resource. The right to pass on to others that which he has legitimately acquired flows directly from this proposition. Some of these arguments may not be persuasive, but can it really be maintained that socialist arguments for just acquisition are morally superior? Most of these maintain the moral fiction that the 'community' can somehow own valued objects, a proposition that, in practice, has subverted not only the morality of individual freedom but also those individualistic mechanisms that power the exchange system.

Irrespective of these more substantive liberal considerations in favour of the free market, one important indirect political implication of the classical liberal version of the Invisible Hand theorem is scarcely considered at all by the critics. This is the view that we cannot simply choose *any* distribution of property rights, since the choice is likely to have unintended consequences that are impossible to foresee. This argument derives from the anti-rationalist version of the Invisible Hand theory and presses home the case that there are self-correcting mechanisms at work—not merely in the market economy but in the legal and social system generally—that produce outcomes which an unaided reason is powerless to improve upon. The evolving Common Law system has historically been quite successful in co-ordinating individual actions. It is because of our ignorance that we cannot plan the future and, therefore, in an indirect utilitarian sense, it is advisable to accept inherited institutions. This view would dispose us then towards accepting a received system of property rights, which has mostly developed accidentally, rather than planning them anew according to an arbitrarily imposed abstract principle.

Although the extension of the Invisible Hand theory appears to involve a descent into an uncritical traditionalism, which is too conservative for more egalitarian *market* economists, its importance in the debate about the institutional framework within which market exchanges take place is frequently over-looked. Even those who favour free exchange and production for the satisfaction of *individual* wants (such as the 'market socialist' thinkers since the 1930s down to some present-day Fabian writers) blithely presuppose that property rights can be shuffled and reshuffled endlessly so as to produce a socialist Pareto-optimal end-state without adverse effects on the institutional framework of economic society.

It is true that the 'distributive question' will remain for the theorists of the Invisible Hand no matter how persuasive the arguments for the higher productivity of the market. The purest versions of the theory maintain a perhaps unacceptable silence over distributive questions while those who suggest principles to modify possibly catastrophic outcomes of an exchange process are (unwittingly) undermining the foundations of the whole theory. The problem may indeed be one for political philosophy rather than political economy. Nevertheless, the work of political economy has had one salutary effect on the wilder extremes of egalitarian political philosophy. It has demonstrated that from a welfare point of view one should look for policies that increase the well-being of everybody, including (and especially) the worst-off, rather than equality for its own sake. Yet it is an obsession with the ideal form of distribution of a 'given' social cake that has characterised much of ethical and political philosophy in the 20th century.

IX. SELF-INTEREST THE UNIVERSAL PRIME-MOVER

The major postulate of Invisible Hand theory, that benign social outcomes are likely to emerge from a social and economic process powered by self-interest alone, has come under attack from a variety of sources. The most recent is in the late Fred Hirsch's famous book, *Social Limits to Growth*.[1] Here the criticism is not so much directed against the 'immorality' of self-interest but against the claim that it is sufficient to satisfy the wants of basically selfish people. Hirsch made much of the phenomenon of 'positional goods', by which he meant goods, such as rare works of art or uncrowded beaches, whose supply cannot be expanded with an increase in demand. It is maintained by Hirsch's followers that as an economy grows the problem of positional goods will be exacerbated. Hirsch assumed that the unrestrained operation of the Invisible Hand would produce a mass of unsatisfiable desires.

Perhaps the novelty of the concept has been exaggerated. It also seems inconsistent with a basic proposition of economic theory: that the supply of most wanted goods is elastic—at a price. If there are such things as positional goods they have always been with us and, presumably, always will; their existence does not point to the failure of the Invisible Hand but to *unalterable scarcity* in the world. It seems to me that Professor Frank Hahn has it about right when he suggests that the market will always provide an adequate supply (and immense variety) of augmentable goods;[2] which makes the problem of positional goods less pressing than is sometimes supposed. The claim sometimes made that it can be alleviated only by the alteration of people's wants has an unduly depressing (and faintly sinister) ring to it.

Is the pursuit of self-interest counter-productive?

There is, however, in anti-market theory a further argument that the pursuit of self-interest is counter-productive: that rational

---

[1] Routledge and Kegan Paul, London, 1977.

[2] Hahn, 'Reflections on the Invisible Hand', *op. cit.*, p. 9.

individuals cannot achieve their undeniably selfish ends by the pursuit of self-interest alone. It is claimed that certain kinds of non-selfish behavioural motivations, such as 'team spirit' or 'loyalty', both of which may require individuals to sacrifice immediately beneficial opportunities, are essential in order to generate the prosperity that is supposed to be a product of unalloyed egoism. Professor Sen cites the post-war Japanese commercial success as partly due to a peculiar ethos, based on traditional notions of obedience and self-sacrifice to the good of the enterprise, which has little to do with the individualistic spirit of Adam Smith.[1] This criticism of self-interest neither damages the Invisible Hand theory nor drastically undermines the assumptions used by its expositors. Universal self-interest is not a logically necessary feature of that theory: it claims only that a social order will emerge from the spontaneous actions of individuals without the necessity for an all-powerful central institution. The importance of the self-interest proposition is that it shows how the public interest is an accidental and unintended outcome of private actions, so that the appeal to a deliberate altruism is either redundant or positively harmful. As Adam Smith remarked: 'I have never known much good done by those who affected to trade for the public good'.

General reliance on the postulate of self-interest to explain economic behaviour does not exclude the possibility that efficient orders may be produced by arrangements that rely on other motivations. A natural process will select in an evolutionary manner the successful industrial forms, and they may well include some that are characterised by non-egoistic motivations. Nineteenth-century and recent history is replete with examples of such *voluntary* action: workers' co-operatives, mutual aid associations for welfare, and church involvement in the original establishment of schools and hospitals. The joint-stock firm itself is a response to the uncertainties of economic life, and we cannot know in advance of experience which is the most efficient mode of its operation. In principle it is no more than a bundle of property rights exercised by individuals. How these individuals use their property rights will depend on the ends they wish to pursue and the constraints they may wish to impose on their actions. No central body can know better than decentralised agents the appropriate form of economic organisation.

[1] Sen, 'The Profit Motive', *op. cit.*, pp. 14-15.

Co-operative enterprise cannot be forced

Certainly, the critics cannot use the examples of (Japanese or other) enterprises that depend less on self-interest and are still successful as a licence to inculcate *deliberately* a non-egoistic spirit in the West. Where this has been tried the results have been disastrous: a long line from Robert Owen's New Lanark experiment through to Anthony Wedgwood Benn's motor-cycle co-operative and the Scottish *Daily News* attests to this simplistic error. The characteristic overlooked when examples of success-ful 'team-spirit' enterprises are cited, is precisely that the institutional arrangements and psychological attitudes said to be the causal factors in these success stories have developed spon-taneously. Where they have not so developed the traditional concept of man as a maximiser is still the only serviceable economic notion we have: strong enough, in practice, to feed and clothe most of the world's population.

Few of the politically liberal Invisible Hand theorists ever supposed that a society could function entirely by selfish impulses. The prevalent view has been that, although the coherence of the market order could be explained by this postulate, the social and legal context in which trading takes place depends on a measure of self-restraint and moral probity that *appears* to be excluded by the psychological assumptions of classical theory. But, of course, such apparently selfless behavioural traits are not excluded. All that is excluded is the construction by a long list of thinkers from Marx to Eric Hobsbawm of rationalistic moral codes which presuppose that man can be other than he is, or envisage that a new altruistic man, unfettered by the ethics of greed, will emerge if only capitalist institutions can be overturned in a revolutionary manner.

There is no externality problem here—the market has not failed to produce the public good of morality and self-restraint. *Laissez-faire* economic arrangements are quite consistent with the traditional Western ethical values of honesty, fair-dealing, justice, and individual autonomy. The non-obligatory virtues of benevolence and charity flourish under capitalist systems. There is evidence of much more selfishness and brutality in socialist régimes precisely because the market—the one activity where egoism can beneficially assert itself—has been suppressed.

[69]

X. POLITICAL *v.* ECONOMIC PROCESS

None of this argument is sufficient to establish an *identity* between spontaneous order theory and liberal political economy. All process theory shows is that there are regularities in the social and economic world which are not captured by end-state theories. There is, however, much practical value in allowing the quasi-natural processes to go on undisturbed, since social and economic orders of more complexity than those that could be consciously designed by man will emerge in this way. It is also true that regularised complex, aggregate phenomena can emerge in a spontaneous manner and yet be undesirable from a liberal or any other political point of view. The most fervent spontaneous order theorist would not deny, for example, that the Common Law has to be supplemented by statute on some occasions.

As has been noted above (pp. 56-57), where large numbers of people are adversely affected by pollution and damage to the environment, satisfactory solutions may be impossible within traditional legal rules: because of immense transaction costs spontaneous legal processes (private law) may break down and 'efficiency' gains may be possible through collective action. But even here it may be possible to devise legal rules that facilitate co-ordination between individuals rather than impose some collective solution. In the logically similar cases of public goods, such as defence, which cannot be priced by the market because 'free-riders' cannot be made to pay for their defence, it has always been accepted by Invisible Hand theorists that there is a necessary role for the state. But this argument does not license wholesale interventionism. In Professor Robert Sugden's delightful words:

> 'like the US Cavalry in a good Western, the government stands ready to rush to the rescue whenever the market "fails", and the economist's job is to advise it on when and how to do so'.[1]

---

[1] R. Sugden, *The Economics of Rights, Co-operation and Welfare*, Blackwell, Oxford, 1986, p. 7.

The political process versus the market process

Two forms of social and political theory, although normative in the sense that they prescribe forms of supposedly desirable public conduct rather than unfold neutral explanatory causal laws of social behaviour, nevertheless have important affinities with the social process model. The first is the system of *liberal political* economy described by classical liberals since Adam Smith. The second is simply 'politics', interpreted not merely as a detached, quasi-scientific study of political phenomena but as a *desirable* decision-making method. This is a view espoused by *'pluralists'* such as Bernard Crick in his *In Defence of Politics*,[1] and perhaps by a majority of students of political science: that crucial social issues should be settled by political methods rather than by the processes of law or economics.

There are difficulties within both approaches. Although I shall show a preference for liberal political economy over politics, I shall keep within the boundaries of ethically neutral analysis by exploring the implications of both independently of personal political philosophy. The two approaches are different, but there are sufficient similarities to make comparisons significant. They can be seen in their common antipathy to end-state theories.

All end-state theories display a fatal weakness: the failure to explain how the desirable outcomes are to be brought about. It is this embarrassing lacuna in each end-state structure that makes it plausible to suggest that they license dictatorship.

Furthermore, both liberal political economy and politics convey, in theory, a certain kind of *neutrality* and *anonymity*. Neutrality is meant in the sense of relative indifference to the particular outcomes of processes: it simply suggests that these processes co-ordinate human action and maximise freedom more effectively than a dictatorship, however benign, Anonymity is the requirement that the processes should confer benefits indiscriminately on the members of an organised community. It is here that politics fares very badly in comparison with liberal political economy.

Liberal political economy or liberalism does not refer to the doctrine of an existing Liberal political party: indeed, throughout the Western world, Liberal political parties espouse agenda roughly the opposite of what I have in mind. By liberalism I simply mean that system of political and economic organisation

---

[1] Penguin Books, Harmondsworth, 1964.

in which individuals co-operate through the exchange of property rights (including their labour) for their mutual benefit. The public interest is understood to be the incidental outcome of private activities rather than the deliberate product of political initiative. Where such political action is unavoidable, as in the supply of public goods, it should be conducted under strict constitutional rules to avoid, or at least minimise, abuse. In a political sense, liberalism is *constitutionalism*: more particularly, political rulers should be subject to *laws not of their own making*. Liberal political economy is the science of spontaneous processes plus the normative (what 'should be') theory of individualist institutions. What interests me is not the existence of such an order in the present world, which is rare, nor its survival, which is problematic, but its intellectual rationale. I am not even concerned with its virtues but with how it can be explained. It has had relatively few genuine supporters in the history of political and economic thought: the gentle caress of Adam Smith's Invisible Hand has always been interpreted in more pugilistic terms by social theorists from Malthus to Keynes (and beyond). Nevertheless, its fiercest critics have paid it the backhanded compliment of extensive refutation.

The most famous contemporary exponent of liberal political economy is F. A. Hayek, and *one* of his major justifications of the market economic-legal order is directly relevant here. This is his attempt to explain it entirely in process terms,[1] which derives from his anti-rationalism: so fragile an instrument is human reason that Hayek relies instead on the forces of social evolution to produce benign social order. The immanent wisdom of tradition is to be preferred to the limited creative powers of the human mind. Those *institutions* (*not* persons) that have survived a neo-Darwinian process of competition will therefore have that durability on which a predictable order depends. The liberal order is then *not* a product of the human mind but a kind of spontaneous mutation: unpredictable, unplanned and undesigned. But, as Hayek is well aware, even when it does occur, it is not particularly durable but subject to various genetic disorders.

It is true that economic processes may be said to develop in an evolutionary manner. The forces of competition do weed out inefficient business enterprises, and firms 'mutate' in an unpredictable manner; yet a certain kind of order is spontaneously

1 F. A. Hayek, *Rules and Order*, Vol. I of *Law, Legislation and Liberty*, Routledge and Kegan Paul, London, 1973.

generated. This is because there is a mechanism, the price system, which ensures a more or less automatic allocative process. But there is no equivalent mechanism to guarantee the spontaneous evolution of those institutions which are necessary to service liberal political economy. Again, institutions and rules which are unplanned may not always be beneficial because sometimes traditional procedures may impede the smooth functioning of a market.

A sovereign parliament leads to decline of liberalism

In Britain the institution of a sovereign parliament, a legislature unlimited by higher law, is perhaps the single most important factor in the decline of its liberal political economy; yet it was not planned: it emerged spontaneously. It is, of course, the growth of statute law that has attenuated the Common Law during this century. This phenomenon rests upon the unproven assumption that Common Law cannot develop rules spontaneously to solve some of the familiar co-ordination problems of modern economies. Ironically, the principle of parliamentary sovereignty is itself a rule of the Common Law.

One important theoretical reason why liberal market orders show a tendency to degeneration has been explained in much detail by public choice theory. This is the argument that the motivations of public officials, elected or appointed, are no different from those of ordinary market transactors, that is, they are no less self-interested. Thus, we cannot assume that officials will maximise the public interest without some incentive.[1] In the public sector there are no such incentives. Although bureaucrats do not maximise 'profits' they do seek the 'rents' that accrue to their monopolistic occupations. In this context 'economic rent' is the difference between the income earned by officials in the public sector and their best alternative in the private sector. Public sector unions keep those rents high by preventing competition determining wages.

In a similar way, democratic processes do not guarantee that the outputs of government will reflect a genuine public interest. On the assumption that politicians desire to be re-elected, party programmes will contain policies that appeal to electorally-significant groups. These will be subsidies to declining industries, tax advantages to specific groups and other exemptions from the rule of law. Each voter will have an incentive to vote for

[1] W. Niskanen, *Bureaucracy: Servant or Master?*, Hobart Paperback 5, IEA, London, 1973.

the party that maximises his group privileges, because the benefits from them are immediate and tangible, rather than for a party that maximises the public interest, the advantages of which are long-term and thinly spread across the population. The competitive nature of unrestrained modern democracy therefore encourages an increase in public spending to pay for the 'bribes' required for electoral success.

Hayek is, of course, aware of all this, and has spent the last 20 years of his life devising elaborate constitutional schemes (a type of genetic engineering, if you like) to prevent the degeneration of the liberal order.[1] Thus it appears that a precocious and presumptuous reason, having been so summarily dismissed, makes a surreptitious re-appearance. Is a designed constitution then simply a liberal end-state? No, it is simply a set of rules in the absence of which the game cannot be played. It could perhaps be described as a 'beginning state'. It is still, if it is liberal, *neutral* between the players.

Nevertheless, this resort to constitutional disciplines points to a serious problem for the theory of liberalism. For does it not give up a part of its claim to neutrality if it licenses the imposition of a set of individualistic rules on the people? Although the operation of such rules permits a variety of outcomes, setting up a 'beginning state' in most circumstances does entail the obliteration of some choices. The only way to make liberalism entirely consistent with pure process theory would be to make its implementation conditional upon *unanimous* agreement. Yet if we make liberalism turn upon unanimity it rapidly ceases to have any connection with the traditional doctrine or, indeed, with the real world.

What all this does show is that it is a chimera to suppose that liberal political economy, no matter how desirable, can be generated by process alone: politics must come in somewhere. Nevertheless, I maintain that the liberal ideal of constitutionalism retains some superiority over the conception of politics as an *exclusive* decision-making method.

---

[1] Hayek, *The Political Order of a Free People*, Vol. III of *Law, Legislation and Liberty*, Routledge and Kegan Paul, London, 1979.

XI. THE IDEOLOGY OF THE POLITICAL PROCESS

Thus I now turn to politics. I shall treat it as a process: a method of making certain sorts of decisions. Although it aims to be neutral about *particular* outcomes, in that those who speak for the virtues of politics do not claim it necessarily produces some 'objective' social good, many political scientists argue that of all possible processes the political one accords most readily with generally held concepts of order and stability. This may be called the 'ideology' of political science. The virtue of politics does not of course follow logically from the study of politics itself, which can claim to be value-free, like any other science. Nevertheless, it is a contingent fact that very many practitioners of political science believe in this particular virtue. The argument I contest is that political activity is generally beneficial in some utilitarian sense, and that it ought to be subject to little formal constraint by constitutional rules that protect private rights.

There is, of course, the perennial question: What is politics? It is perhaps an 'essentially contested concept' which defies exact and non-controversial application. Nevertheless, I will risk the charge of arbitrariness and identify two types of politics: *technological* politics and *group* politics. Technological politics goes along with end-state theories. Some desirable outcome is 'objectively' determined and the best technical means available are used to implement it. Thus rational planners (Keynesian or otherwise) calculate a general equilibrium and 'command' it, in the sense that they hope to produce some kind of economic plan. In a similar manner social welfare functions embodying utility or social justice are specified and implemented. And we have said enough to indicate that the absence of any procedural considerations in these theories leaves them defenceless against the charge that they depend on the existence of omniscient and benevolent rulers. This is to leave aside the question of the objectivity of the end-state judgement itself.

Group theories are anti-rationalist

Group theories of politics are not guilty of these errors: indeed, they are implicitly directed against the rationalism of end-state theories. The group theory, or pluralism, in opposition to the imposition of desirable outcomes, recommends as desirable that result which emerges from the interplay of groups in society, operating through both a democratic voting procedure and a less formalised bargaining process. Professor Bernard Crick writes:

'Politics . . . can be simply defined as the activity by which differing interests within a given unit of rule are conciliated by giving them a share of power in proportion to their importance to the welfare and survival of the whole community. And, to complete the definition, a political system is that type of government where politics. proves successful in ensuring reasonable stability and order.'[1]

Politics, like economics, claims Crick, is concerned with allocational problems (who gets what) and, like market processes, political processes do not determine some objective good, say, of justice or efficiency. Here is Crick again:

'Politics are, as it were, the market place and the price mechanism of all social demands—though there is no guarantee that a just price will be struck.'[2]

For example, under 'politics' individuals are not paid their marginal product; they get what their group can bargain for them.

This seems to me to be a reasonably accurate description of the type of politics that goes on in the governmental systems of Western democracies. What is lacking is any real recognition of the obvious truth that political processes invariably result in *collective* decisions, which are binding on the whole community. Thus, while political processes are characterised by freedom and diversity, their outcomes are still coercive, categorical, and final.

So much for the description of the process; what of its virtues? The ordinary man in the street tends to regard politics as an unpleasant necessity (akin to an estate agency). It is alien to justice, truth and morality, yet something we cannot do without. Many social scientists and journalists write anodyne books and articles to prove the opposite, that the political process is required for a very wide range of human activities and that it has a special kind of virtue. I tend to think that the ordinary man in the street may be roughly right (although he is wrong about estate agents, who are simply the bearers of tacit knowledge).

Political processes are assumed, without much thought or

[1] B. Crick, *In Defence of Politics, op. cit.*, p. 21.   [2] *Ibid.*, pp. 22-23.

evidence, to be in the public interest: politics is said to be not a mindless playing of a game for its own sake but a procedure from which some benefit will result, at least in comparison to other processes, such as markets. But it is easy to show that politics, where this means the reconciliation of pressure groups, is not a necessary beneficial activity even under the most favourable circumstances. As the economist Mancur Olson has well put it:

> 'It does not follow that the results of pressure group activity would be harmless, much less desirable, even if the balance of power equilibrium resulting from the multiplicity of pressure groups kept any one pressure group from getting out of line. *Even if such a pressure group system worked with perfect fairness to every group, it would still tend to work inefficiently.*'[1]

Pressure groups and free trade

Unrestrained pressure-group activity may produce results favourable to the members of a group but unfavourable to the society as a whole; which consists of no more than the collectivity of group members. To illustrate this simple, but often misunderstood proposition, I will take the case of protectionism. From the point of view of the consumer and society as a whole, it is clear that free trade between nations is the optimal economic policy since citizens as consumers gain from the efficiencies brought about by the international division of labour. From the point of view of any single producer group it would be better if their products were protected by tariffs from foreign competition while all other goods were allowed to come in freely. For government to protect merely one group would, of course, be bad politics, leaving aside the question of 'fairness', since it would mean ignoring other groups equally 'essential' for the welfare of the community. Yet to satisfy all the groups by protective measures would make society as a whole, that is to say, the group members taken individually, worse off than they would be under free trade.

Politics, in practice, produces Prisoners' Dilemmas: situations in which rational self-interest leads to outcomes not desired by anybody. As Michael James has pointed out,[2] Olson's expla-

---

[1] M. Olson, *The Logic of Collective Action*, Harvard University Press, Cambridge, Mass., 1965, p. 124.

[2] M. James, *Parliament and the Public Interest*, Australian Institute for Public Policy, Perth, 1985, p. 34.

[77]

nation of group politics is a perfect case of Rousseau's famous distinction between the *will of all*, what everybody votes for individually, and the *General Will*, what they would vote for as their common interests if only they could be so motivated. There are, of course, Prisoners' Dilemmas in market society, notably in the supply of public goods, but it seems to me that the continual and unnecessary politicisation of economic and social life produces many more. For it creates incentives for groups to invest in politics and other re-distributive activities ('rent-seeking') rather than production—to the ultimate detriment of everybody. To quote Olson again, pressure groups behave like 'wrestlers struggling over the contents of a china shop'.[1]

In the real world of contemporary politics, as distinct from the ideal vision of pluralism, things are different, perhaps even worse. This is because in most political systems, groups are unequally balanced; some gain significantly more than others from government privilege and exemptions from the rule of law. In my example of protectionism, the producer groups were roughly equal, so that the gains free trade would bring them are immediate and discernible. In such circumstances they may have just sufficient an incentive to contract their way out of this group version of the Hobbesian 'war of all against all'. They could agree unanimously to lay down their politically deter-mined privileges and immediately benefit. In reality *some* groups, because their gains from politics are so large, would have no incentive to make such a deal because it would in the event harm them. The classical example here is that of farmers (or more probably landowners, who secure rent from farmers). So extensive are their accumulated gains from the myriad of price support schemes, subsidies and tariffs which Western govern-ments have made available that it is highly unlikely that the gains from universal free trade would compensate them for the loss of their privileges.

In *The Rise and Decline of Nations* Olson argues to telling effect, and no little irony, that political stability, so much admired by pluralists, is in the real world harmful—at least in terms of economic growth rates. For it is this relative tranquility that enables groups to solidify and entrench themselves. Olson claims that those Western countries which have experienced social upheavals during this century—Japan, France, Western Germany and so on—have enjoyed faster growth rates precisely

[1] Olson, *The Rise and Decline of Nations*, Yale University Press, New Haven, 1982, p. 44.

because the upheavals caused the disintegration of politically powerful groups. The period of the German 'social market economy', which lasted from 1950 to the late 1960s, is a spectacular example.

Constitutional reform v. 'elective dictatorship'

In contrast, Britain is peculiarly disadvantaged in having very few constraints on the process of politics. The co-existence of a sovereign parliament and an electoral system that enables a government to be formed with considerably less than half the support of the electorate encourages parties to appeal to 'rainbow' coalitions of minorities rather than to the public interest. It is significant that this constitutional *ancien régime* is fervently supported by the leaderships of the two major political parties in this country: there is no stronger admirer of Britain's unreformed constitution than Mrs Thatcher.

There is a certain irony about the attitude of Conservative politicians to constitutional reform. Throughout the 1974-79 period of Labour rule, many of them protested about 'elective dictatorship': a system which permitted a government elected by a minority of the people to use the full powers of parliamentary sovereignty to implement unpopular social and economic policies. Many of these policies, especially the extension of trade union immunities, were dictated by pressure groups. Conservative politicians and academic lawyers, in response to such action, pressed for proportional representation; and a Bill of Rights that would take the protection of individual liberties (although economic liberties were rarely included) out of parliamentary politics. However, since 1979 there has been some progress towards reversing collectivism under the very same system of 'elective dictatorship'. Not surprisingly, Conservative politicians now adopt a Trappist-like silence on the constitution.

The response of some liberal political economists is to say that, if the present constitutional arrangements remain, this progress is liable to be reversed in the future. They are then prepared to accept stricter constitutional rules, perhaps a two-thirds majority rule for parliament, which would undoubtedly slow up the process of liberalisation, but would make the present achievements more secure. Economic liberals prefer permanent constitutional rules to reliance on electoral serendipity. Nevertheless, it must be conceded that such constitutional reform proposals seem fanciful at present.

This brief examination of political processes then presents the Invisible Hand theorists with something of a problem. For the apparently random processes of the politics of pluralism do resemble in important ways some of the features of the market that anti-rationalists admire: the paraphernalia of voting systems, bargaining between groups and the inter-play of ideas in open societies surely prevent the implementation of 'rational plans' or designs. The political systems of Western democracies do display a certain kind of 'orderliness' which may be seen as analogous to the order of unplanned markets. Indeed, the parallel becomes more enticing when it is realised that the theorists of the Invisible Hand of the market do not normally claim that it produces 'efficiency' (at least, not in some kind of engineering sense). Its major merit is said to lie in its ability to co-ordinate human actions and to guarantee an order of predictability through time rather than to produce some static *nirvana*. Is not politics like this? What is it about the market that makes it superior, as its protagonists claim?

No price mechanism in politics

It is here that the aforementioned differences between markets and politics become relevant: the absence of an equivalent to the price mechanism in politics. The price system is a *natural* phenomenon whereas the rules that govern political processes are to a very large extent *artifices*: and even if they have developed spontaneously, as with parliamentary sovereignty in Britain, there is certainly no guarantee that they will service the order of freedom. It is for this reason that a genuine con-stitutionalism is so important for liberal political economy.

In the past, liberal political economists did not inquire into the nature of the state; it was treated as an exogenous institution or agency which, because of the universality of its rules and its monopoly of legitimate power, was admirably suited to supply public goods and solutions to other types of market 'failure'. The recognition that it is not a mere automaton which implements rational designs but is an institution manned by flesh-and-blood individuals who have interests of their own that may not coincide with the interests of an anonymous public is one of the most important achievements of modern political economy. The demand for strict constitutional rules to constrain the processes of politics can then be seen as the demand for some surrogate for the principles of profit and loss that naturally constrain economic

[80]

agents. What is especially important about a 'monetary constitution', including a balanced-budget rule and a 'monetary rule' to prevent inflation, is that it enables the Invisible Hand of the market to clasp the Invisible Hand of politics in more friendly a fashion. Such institutional constraints can then be seen as imperfect surrogates for the automatic constraint of price that exists in unplanned markets.

Discretionary political decisions harm efficiency and freedom

If large parts of social and economic life become subject to discretionary political decisions, as they are in Britain today, there are malign consequences for freedom and order. It is certainly true, as the pluralists maintain, that political activity does itself necessitate some liberties—the freedom to associate, organise, campaign and persuade. It is also true that such activity generates competition between groups and, of course, ideas. But what is undeniable is that the results of a group process of politics are always categorical decisions that apply to the whole community; they are coercive.

If the procedural rules under which such activity operates are flimsy and impose few constraints on what can be implemented coercively, and if they do not compel political decision-makers to represent a very wide section of the community (in Britain, all governments, with *rare* exceptions, are minority governments), deleterious consequences follow for both efficiency and freedom. Efficiency is affected because political decisions disrupt the flow of tacit knowledge on which economic co-ordination depends: they are *final* and *decisive* and therefore prevent the experimentation in problem-solving that continually takes place by decentralised agents in open-market societies. Solutions to scientific, economic and legal problems, for example, are not found by political methods with lobbying, majority voting, and short-term horizons. Centralised political decisions will reflect only a partial view of knowledge.

The effect of an over-extended range of politics on freedom should be obvious: it elevates the public world over the private world; it replaces personal choice by collective choice. It seems to be an unchallenged assumption of the 20th century that social problems can be solved only by political, coercive measures. But many of our personal and social relationships are literally 'anarchic': that is, governed by internalised rules and conven-

[81]

tions rather than by commands. They are conducted more 'efficiently' for that very reason.

None of this discussion is meant to encourage the fantasy that there can be a world without politics. I have indicated that both end-state and process models of society are deficient to the extent that their analyses reflect a lack of understanding of public decision-making. What the discussion does suggest is that the pluralists are wrong in claiming that all forms of social order depend on politics: there are co-ordinating processes that are going on all the time in society, most notably in economics, law and, of course, science. That such activity goes on in a context of politics (with the ultimate long-stop of coercion) does not justify the conclusion that politics should be unlimited in its range.

The type of politics that is most appropriate to freedom, understood as both an instrumental and ethical value, is *constitutional* politics, a system in which more or less fixed rules (which can secure much more general support than that offered by collections of groups) provide guidelines for decentralised agents. Furthermore, a constitution should not be seen as a kind of transmission rule which turns individual preferences into collective decisions; as is the majority-rule procedure. For there is no such rule which can effect such a transmission without contradictions and paradoxes. And even if this could be done it would simply permit a series of impositions of alternative end-states. A constitution is not a transmission rule; it is a set of *constraints*. In Mr Nevil Johnson's felicitous expression: 'A constitution is indeed a corset for those who seek power'.[1]

Those who study politics should carefully distinguish between politics as an *activity* and politics as a *discipline*. This the pluralists fail to do. For the objective study of politics, of governments, voting, parliaments and so on does not commit us to the 'ideology' of political science, the view that political decisions have a special kind of moral priority.

[1] N. Johnson, *In Search of the Constitution*, Pergamon Press, Oxford, 1977, p. 147.

XII. CONCLUSION

The brief analysis of this *Hobart Paper* suggests that economists, political scientists and political philosophers should be concerned with showing how institutional re-arrangements might assist in the working of the Invisible Hand. Too many economists have been guilty of gleefully demonstrating how existing market structures depart from an hypothetical optimum. Political scientists too often imagine that the only way to avoid dictatorship is to let politics operate in a more or less unrestrained manner irrespective of the damage it can do to the efficiency properties of the market.

But if there is no Invisible Hand process there are no economic regularities, no predictable patterns or signals by which individuals can organise their lives, and no 'science' of human conduct. In the absence of the Invisible Hand, and in the decline of the constitutional constraints that must govern all individual action, the economic world becomes the plaything of, initially (and very briefly), the delicate, elegant but headily unrealistic abstract theorist, and then the defenceless target of unconstrained political authority.

TOPICS FOR GENERAL DISCUSSION
AND QUESTIONS FOR STUDENTS

1. Distinguish between 'end-state' and 'process' theories of politico-economic society. Assess their strengths and weaknesses.

2. Which of the two theories better explains developments in the industrial West, Eastern Europe and the Far East?

3. What is the importance of their contrasting conceptions of 'equilibrium'?

4. Evaluate the 'end-state' theory of utilitarianism. Does it illuminate present-day developments in any part of the world?

5. What is the contribution of the 'end-state' theory of 'social justice' to understanding present-day society?

6. Analyse the 'process' theory of politico-economic society. Assess its relevance and limitations in explaining the difference between market-based and state-directed economies.

7. What is the contribution of mathematics to the notion of 'equilibrium'? In what ways has it helped and hindered the development of the concept as a means of explaining the real world?

8. What is the role of the entrepreneur in market-based and state-directed economies?

9. Compare and contrast the results produced by 'the invisible hand' in the market process and the political process.

10. Discuss the benefits and defects of the profit motive in the market and the power motive in politics.

[84]

11. In what ways, if any, is human nature changed in passing from the market process to the political process, and *vice versa.*

12. What role, if any, would you assign constitutional limitations on government in the political process? What regulatory or other limitations would you put on the market process?

READINGS FOR FURTHER STUDY

Barry, N. P., 'The Tradition of Spontaneous Order', *Literature of Liberty*, Vol. V, 1982, pp. 7-59.

An historical account of the development of Invisible Hand social theory.

Buchanan, J. M., *The Limits of Liberty: Between Anarchy and Leviathan*, University of Chicago Press, Chicago, 1975.

An excellent theoretical explanation of the need for constitutional restraint on government.

Flew, A., *The Politics of Procrustes*, Temple Smith, London, 1981.

Philosophically sophisticated but hard-hitting critique of all varieties of egalitarianism and social justice.

Hahn, F. H., *Equilibrium and Macroeconomics*, Blackwell, Oxford, 1984.

Contains many of Hahn's most lucid essays.

Hayek, F. A., *Individualism and Economic Order*, Routledge and Kegan Paul, London, 1948.

Contains a number of pioneering essays on the theory of market process plus a critique of market socialism.

——, *Studies in Philosophy, Politics and Economics*, Routledge and Kegan Paul, London, 1967.

Contains many of Hayek's finest essays on the methodology of the social sciences.

Johnson, N., *In Search of the Constitution*, Pergamon Press, Oxford, 1977.

Though now a little out of date this book is still a fine account of the constitutional decay of Great Britain in the 1960s and 1970s.

[86]